Why Not You?
The Old Man's Guide to Prosperity

Art Merrill

Table of Contents

CHAPTER ONE
PITAs

It was a year to the day since his Millie had passed away. He missed her dearly and deeply.

Many times, he had heard people say that when loved ones die, a part of you dies with them. He had considered it to be just one of those things people say to the grieving, like "they are in a better place now" or "they are not in pain anymore".

He had been wrong. When the cancer took her away, it had indeed taken away a piece of him.

When they met, she immediately reached right through his cool exterior and extracted a tiny piece of him that was warm and vulnerable. A piece of him that no one before her had seen and that he himself hadn't even known existed. She had taken it and nurtured it. She had bathed it in the sunlight that naturally shone from her very soul.

She had grown that tiny piece into a fully formed man she kept for herself, as most people had never met him. He'd become like a perfect imaginary friend to her, but he was very real indeed. When she got cancer, so did he. He missed her, losing that part of himself had compounded his grief several times over. He missed her and the person he had been when he was with her.

It had been a year now since they'd both left him, and he'd planned to spend this day in fond remembrance. He was going to light their favorite candles, listen to some of their favorite music, even cook their favorite meal. That was the plan.

As it turned out, none of that was going to happen.

Hollis Haynes had been living in the same house on the same street for over forty years.

Most of his original neighbors had passed away or moved on. To his dismay, they were replaced by more families and many more houses.

Despite never having had any children of his own, he intellectually understood why they must exist, but must they all live on his street? It seemed like the children far outnumbered the adults, whom he rarely saw. He wasn't entirely convinced that all these kids even had parents.

He had given up trying to learn their names long ago. Instead, had given them a single nickname, which he mostly kept to himself. He called them PITAs. PITA, of course, stood for Pain in The Ass.

Nevertheless, here he was. One of the biggest PITAs of all, his neighbor's ten-year old son, was inside his house, sitting on his couch, on a Saturday, for the next eight hours at least.

The conversation with his neighbor that left them here was a blur to him. It had happened too fast for him to process properly, but he remembered bits and pieces of it. He'd heard something about a work schedule change. Something else about no one else could help her. Some other apparently pertinent details and a barrage of "please", "just this once", and "I will owe you one." He still couldn't recall the exact point in the conversation where he had agreed to watch the kid, but he clearly had agreed to do so. The evidence had knocked on his door at eight a.m. sharp.

Having never raised any children himself, he was unsure how to entertain one for a full day. He did know, however, that these young creatures liked to eat, so he figured he would start with that. Food he could provide well, for even though he was a light eater and didn't entertain very often, he firmly believed in keeping a well-stocked pantry and refrigerator for when he did have guests. Having had some food availability issues as a child, he had perhaps overcompensated as an adult. He wasn't prone to over-eating himself, but he was prone to over-feeding others. He led the boy into the kitchen and watched in amazement as the boy casually and quickly dismissed option after option offered to him by Mr. Haynes.

Eventually Hollis let the boy rummage through the refrigerator himself. The boy finally settled on a grilled cheese sandwich as his choice. He wasn't exactly impressed with the boy's decision, but it was a decision, so he agreed to make the sandwich for him.

He noticed that the boy was a bit energetic. He couldn't stay seated for any length of time and was constantly fidgeting when he was seated. After he ate, Hollis thought it would be better for the boy to expend his energy outdoors instead of the interior of his home, which was decidedly not designed for children to play in. They walked around the backyard for a while, the young boy seemingly fixated on the centerpiece of the yard, the large inground pool. Apparently, the boy had only seen pools that large in schools and community centers, never in someone's yard.

The boy's mother had wisely packed him a swimsuit and a towel, just in case. Mr. Haynes thought the pool was as good a place as any for the boy to tire himself out. There wasn't much he could break in the pool. He directed the boy to the pool house to change and sat on the edge of the pool at the shallow end, dangling his feet near the stairs. The boy, however, had no intention of entering the pool in such a boring and conventional way. He emerged from the pool house and made a beeline for the diving board at the deep end.

Mr. Haynes watched curiously as the boy bounced several times on the board and finally hit the water with a scream of "cannon ball!" For over two hours, Mr. Haynes supervised as the boy found seemingly endless ways to amuse himself in the pool. When the boy had finally exhausted himself, Mr. Haynes returned to the kitchen to prepare some snacks while the boy went to the pool house to dry off and change.

He brought the tray of snacks to a picnic table near the pool that had an umbrella over it which kept it relatively cool even in the summer heat. As the boy was settling into his chair and eyeing the snack tray, Mr. Haynes felt compelled to make some small talk and asked, "So, how did you end up being my neighbor, anyway?" He wasn't quite prepared for the depth and the breadth of the boy's reply. The boy explained how his parents had divorced a few years ago.

"We moved a few times because we had some trouble paying rent. Mom finally got a new job that pays pretty good, and that's why we moved here. The rent was a little higher, but Mom really wanted to live in a decent neighborhood, even if it meant we would have to struggle a bit. The new job pays well, but sometimes her schedule changes all of a sudden, that's why she needs someone to watch me on Saturdays."

Mr. Haynes listened quietly and felt a bit guilty about his previous judgments of the boy. He was surprised to realize that he hadn't had the urge to yell at the boy once the whole day, something he'd assumed would happen more than once during his visit.

They went inside, and Mr. Haynes decided that the boy could use a little quiet time and sat him on the couch, making a point to guide him towards the end of the couch opposite the spot his wife loved so much. He still liked to leave that spot open, though he wasn't sure why. He handed him the remote control to the large flat screen television and sat at his desk across from the couch and to the side of the television.

Figuring the boy would likely fall asleep watching television, he turned his computer on and pulled up the website that he used to study the charts from which he often made decisions about the stocks he would trade the following Monday morning. He liked to have his strategies planned out before the markets opened and chaos ensued. As often happened, he quickly became lost in the forest of numbers and charts before him.

"Whatcha doing?" The question snapped him out of his fog. He hadn't noticed the boy leave the couch and cross the room to where he now stood, several inches from Mr. Haynes's face and speaking in a voice far louder than necessary from that distance. Mr. Haynes looked at the kid and realized he was expecting an answer.

"I am working on my stock portfolio," he answered, hoping to discourage further questions.

It didn't work.

"What's a stock portfolio?" asked the boy.

He knew the boy had unintentionally asked a question that would require a long answer to properly address, so he tried to dismiss him with the short version. "It's something I do to make money," he answered reluctantly.

"Everyone says you have a lot of money. The other kids say you are the richest man in town.

They say you have a lot of money, but don't give anyone else any of it." "Oh yeah, is that what they say?" Mr. Haynes replied.

"I know a lot about money too," the boy volunteered.

Mr. Haynes chuckled out loud. "What do you know about money, kid?" The boy was starting to annoy him just as he had expected, if a bit behind schedule.

"Money doesn't grow on trees, we can't afford it, Mom isn't made of money, and rich people are greedy!" The boy recited proudly.

Mr. Haynes's smile faded, and his heart sank. He felt an onrush of emotions when he was instantly transported back to the childhood home where he had heard those very phrases almost verbatim thousands of times, mostly from his parents. They were well-intentioned, but their faulty ideas and concepts, planted firmly in his young head, took decades to unlearn.

It was nearly forty years before he was finally able to begin breaking free of their ideas enough to achieve a fair measure of prosperity for himself and his wife. He also knew for a fact that he carried some remnants around with him to this day. He often wondered how far he could have gone if he hadn't spent so many years operating from faulty premises and completely erroneous ideas about money and wealth.

Where would he be if he'd had several more decades to grow and take advantage of all he had learned? The fact was that he could not count on having decades left to find out.

"Hey! did you even hear me?" the kid broke Mr. Haynes out of his daze.

"Yeah, yeah, I heard you, how could I not hear you? Haven't you ever heard of an inside voice?" For the first time, he looked the boy in the eye, and he saw something. He saw just a glimmer of light, a spark that told him that maybe this one kid, just this one, might not be so bad after all.

"You sure do know a lot about money for a kid your age, too bad it is all wrong," Mr. Haynes deadpanned.

"If you know so much, why don't you teach me?" the boy challenged.

In all the years Hollis Haynes had spent in this small town, building his business and then building his wealth, not one of his fellow citizens had ever asked him for wisdom. Many had asked for his money, but not one of them had ever asked him how to make their own, so they wouldn't have to ask for it. Slightly impressed, Mr. Haynes decided to mentally remove this boy, and only this one, from his PITA category. From now on, this PITA would be known as "Tommy."

CHAPTER TWO
The Old Man

As he got ready to head out the door for his usual Sunday session with the Old Man, Hollis found himself unexpectedly distracted. He found himself thinking about Tommy instead of the content of the discussion he was about to have with the Old Man. He saw a lot of himself in the kid. Although he resisted that notion on a conscious level, he was pretty sure he was never that hyperactive, even at Tommy's age.

The Old Man was working on his biggest project to date, and it was the first of his that was not designed to make money. Hollis was fascinated both with the complexity of the project, and how well the Old Man seemed to be handling all the details.

For many years, his mentor had taught him about the importance of giving back and the realization of true prosperity. Listening to these concepts for so long made watching them now manifest themselves before his very eyes an exciting time for them both. Their recent sessions had taken on an air of significance, both because of the scope of the project itself and the reality of the Old Man's ever more obvious mortality.

The Old Man was starting to age more noticeably in the last few years, and he had expressed concerns about living to see this project through to completion.

They never spoke of the possibility out loud, but there was an unspoken sense that the Old Man wasn't sharing every detail of the project with Hollis just for academic purposes, he was preparing him to take over and finish it if he passed away or otherwise became unable to see it through personally. They both understood the sense of urgency, though they never explicitly expressed it. It was simply understood between the mentor and his student.

Now, as he closed his front door and walked towards his car, Hollis waved at his neighbors sitting on their front porch, and it struck him that he hadn't openly acknowledged any of his neighbors in quite some time. He was somewhat saddened at the truth of his own behavior, as he knew that he had become very different when his wife passed.

He had been giving himself a pass as a grieving widower, but now he felt a bit guilty about how he had been acting towards his perfectly innocent fellow citizens. He felt just a little ashamed of himself and he knew the Old Man wouldn't have condoned his behavior either.

Tommy and his mother waved back, though they were visibly surprised by the gesture.

As he turned into the park where they always met, Hollis was mentally struggling to remember exactly where last week's talk had ended. He knew the Old Man wouldn't recap it for him, he would just assume they were on the same page, like they normally were.

They hadn't been talking long before the Old Man noticed how distracted Hollis was. They had known each other for years and Hollis was an open book to him. "All right, spit it out, what's on your mind?" the Old Man asked as he put down the papers he had been referring to and removed his glasses.

"You haven't heard a word I have said for at least five minutes, let's talk about whatever it is so we can get back to this stuff," he said, gesturing towards the pile of documents spread over the picnic table.

"Well, oddly enough, it's one of those kids in the neighborhood," Hollis started.

"One of the PITAs? Oh lord, what did he do to you? Toilet paper your trees? Break your window with a baseball?" volunteered the Old Man.

"Worse than that, he spent the entire day yesterday at my house!" Hollis said.

The Old Man was genuinely taken aback. He was almost certain none of the neighborhood kids had ever seen the interior of Hollis's house except for maybe peering in a window when he wasn't home.

"If I am going to help you, I am going to need more information than that, but I confess, you have my attention." The Old Man pried.

Hollis explained about the mother and the whirlwind conversation he had with her that resulted in him apparently agreeing to watch the kid for just the one day. He relayed the events of the day, including the swimming and the snacks, and the conversation that occurred at the end of the day. He even admitted hinting to the boy's mother that he would be open to watching the kid again if it became necessary.

"I can't figure out exactly why, but this kid didn't get under my skin as much as I expected him to, I don't know what it is about him." Hollis continued.

The Old Man laughed out loud. "Really? You really don't get it? Heck, I figured it out thirty seconds into your story! The kid is you! You don't hate him because you see yourself in him. He is a bright kid whose life circumstances will likely lead him to a life of utter mediocrity, unless he gets as lucky as you did, and stumbles into a mentor like me!" he continued "You have no choice, as far as I can tell. I am not going to live forever, and this project will likely be my last. You must become the Old Man, and the kid must become your student, it is a full circle thing, or something like that."

There was no arguing with the Old Man. Hollis knew instinctively that he was totally right. He had been so caught up in being the student for so long, he hadn't really thought much about becoming the teacher, but it was time to do so, especially because his own mentor would soon be unavailable to him.

Mr. John interrupted him as he processed the meaning of this new mission. "You do know what this means, don't you?" his Old Man asked with a huge grin, "You are now officially the Old Man!"

As he drove away from the park and towards his house, he was unsure how to offer to watch the kid without seeming anxious or overly eager to his mother. He knew that his reputation for disliking kids was well established in his neighborhood. A sudden

9

transformation would seem odd. He waved again as he entered his front door.

He decided to wait a few days before this new Old Man casually asked the mother over the fence between their yards. "Any luck finding someone to watch the kid Saturday?"

She was a little surprised at his concern, but Tommy had told her that he'd had fun with the Old Man, especially swimming in the huge pool and eating his fill of snacks, so she was a little relieved that he wasn't complaining about Tommy.

The truth was, she didn't know anyone nearby because she was new to the area. Tommy was too old for any of the professional daycare type of places, and even if he weren't, the costs would almost make working the extra shifts pointless, as they would almost completely offset what she earned working. Also, she didn't really have the option of declining the work, since the Saturday shifts were simply not something she could refuse if she ever hoped to be promoted.

Leaving Tommy with a neighbor that didn't particularly like kids wasn't the best option, but it was likely the only viable option she had, and he had told her to "let him know" which implied he was open to the idea.

"No, not yet, and I am running out of time." She detailed the challenges involved, and he seemed sympathetic, so she just asked, "Any chance you could keep him just one more time until I can make some other arrangements? I can pay you, but not very much."

"Well, he didn't break anything last Saturday, and I have no plans, so sure, I can watch him, but under one condition. You take whatever you could pay and save that money instead. I couldn't take your money, it just wouldn't be right.

"Maybe I will give Tommy some chores to do or something to earn his keep. Heck, maybe I will even teach him some things about money, so he can take care of his mother someday."

She thanked him profusely, went to tell Tommy the news, and was surprised that Tommy seemed happy about the new development. The Old Man went back inside and spent the rest of the day trying to figure out what his teacher had gotten him into and how the hell he was going to entertain a ten-year old week after week.

CHAPTER THREE
Worldview

For many years now, Hollis had been haunted by a statistic he read in a book. He found it both disturbing and puzzling that in the richest country in the world, a country that many referred to as the wealthiest nation to ever exist, only 5 percent of Americans at age sixty-five were wealthy or at least financially independent. The rest were still working or struggling financially.

How was this possible? He had dedicated most of his adult life to finding the answer to this question. He had found many possible explanations, but none of them sufficiently explained this phenomenon. Many people had difficult circumstances to overcome. Many ran into challenges they couldn't defeat.

There were other factors as well to explain why any one individual failed to achieve prosperity, but was there a common denominator that exacerbated these myriad other factors? What was the one thing that those who failed to reach their full potential shared with each other? What was the most common factor among those who did succeed? What helped the 5 percent overcome the same adversities and challenges that defeated the 95 percent?

The Old Man's exhaustive studies had led him to an inescapable conclusion: Most folks are pre-programmed to fail from childhood! Sadly, parents who struggle and fail to reach their own goals often come to the wrong conclusion when they try to analyze their failures.

They falsely assign blame to many circumstances that may have been challenging but had been overcome by other people too often to have been a valid excuse for their failure.

It was also an interesting fact that the children of prosperous parents usually became prosperous themselves, independent of inheritance or any other obvious advantages they may have had. On the other hand, many of those who failed also had successfully attained a higher education and even high-level jobs and careers. Although they made excellent salaries and owned a fair amount of material goods, they never achieved real wealth or financial independence.

What the Old Man found to be the single most common factor that decided the fate of a person who strived for a better life was quite simple after all. People generally rose or fell according to how they perceived the world. If they believed the world was one of scarcity and tough competition, they usually struggled and failed only a few times before they conceded defeat and settled into a life of mediocrity, forever doomed to dream about what could have been.

If, however, they carried a worldview that convinced them that the world was one of abundance and plenty, they found the strength to persist until they succeeded. If they knew that success was inevitable through the sheer volume of abundance to be had, they continued until they won, no matter how many times they failed before they succeeded.

It was simply a matter of whether you believed there was enough to go around or not, if you believed the better things in life were limited or unlimited in nature.

If his adventure of teaching Tommy about money and wealth was going to be anything other than an exercise in futility, he knew the first thing he would have to address with Tommy was implanting in him an accurate view of the world around him as one of abundance.

He had to help Tommy realize that there was plenty for him to have, even if he had to create it himself. He had to disabuse him of the notion that he had to compete with others for the better things in life. It had taken him decades to defeat the worldview of scarcity that his own parents had inadvertently instilled in him, due to their personal experience surviving severe poverty.

During that difficult time, scarcity was a reality for them, but even then, many fortunes were built by those able to spot opportunities that others missed. He was convinced that in many ways he was still carrying remnants of that faulty programming around with him today.

Nonetheless, he now faced a unique challenge, one that never having his own children left him ill-equipped to handle. He had to completely contradict the boy's short history of experience with struggle and convince him that his experience so far in life was not a harbinger of his future. He had to contradict basically everything the boy's mother had told him and inadvertently taught him, either through her words or her deeds.

He understood how tough this would be, as the boy's mother was a good woman and she was handling her own circumstances quite nobly, as far as he could tell. Unfortunately, the same set of ideas and thoughts that served his parents well during their own hardships was the same set of concepts that were guiding Tommy's mother through her tough times.

What helps you survive during tough times can be what keeps you from moving past those times and into better times. His mentor once told him that "the same umbrella that kept the rain off your back yesterday keeps the sunshine off your shoulders today."

He decided to show Tommy what he wanted him to learn in a way that he could grasp without getting into a long-winded explanation of economics and without criticizing the boy's mother, because that would likely backfire quite quickly.

At eight a.m. sharp, his doorbell rang. He answered the door and let Tommy in. However, he made it clear to Tommy that if he was coming over every Saturday at the same time, he would have to knock and then enter. The Old Man wasn't going to walk to the door every time just to open it for him. That was just a waste of time and energy, neither of which the Old Man possessed in the quantities he had in years past.

After Tommy had chosen a snack from the kitchen and the Old Man had prepared his coffee, he took Tommy out in the backyard to begin his lesson. He pointed to the lawn. "Tommy, do you see that grass right there?" Tommy nodded, still chewing a cookie. "That grass grows every day, doesn't it?" he asked. The boy nodded again. "Even if I do nothing to it, it grows. That is the way the world works, it is always growing and expanding. The trees are the same way, they always grow. There is more wood being created in every tree in every forest in the world."

They sat at the large table by the pool. The Old Man took out the legal pad he had under his arm and drew a small square on it. Tommy was finishing his snack and was paying attention to the Old Man's primitive drawing.

"This square here, Tommy, is a piece of land with nothing on it. Let's say it is worth $20." He saw no reason to bog the boy down with large, but realistic numbers, his point would be clear enough without real numbers. "If I build a house on this land, the house and the land would be worth $120 or so. With me so far?" The boy nodded.

"To build this house, I would have to pay a builder $100, though." It was time to include the boy. "Tommy, if I buy this land for $20, and I pay the builder $100 more to build the house, how much have I spent?"

"$120" came the answer.

"But how much is the land and the property worth now?" asked the Old Man. "$120" the boy repeated.

"Here is where the magic part comes in, Tommy. Do you like magic?" the boy nodded. "That money actually doubled!"

The Old Man explained that when he paid the builder $100, the builder now had $100 to pay other people with and to buy stuff for himself and his family, but the Old Man still had his money, it was just now in the form of a house and land, which were likely worth more than $120. He had turned his $120 into much more, just like magic.

The Old Man had a property worth at least $120, which was what he spent, and the builder also now had $100, and the seller of the land had $20. The Old Man further explained to Tommy whenever people worked and put forth effort, value was created. The world would keep getting more abundant as long as people worked hard.

He told Tommy that if he learned his lessons well and did as the Old Man showed him, there would be plenty of ways for him to perform his own magic and make money from nothing also. The boy smiled and promised to listen very closely to his lessons.

Satisfied that he had the boy's attention and that he could reinforce the notion of abundance over time, he released the boy from the day's lesson and tilted his head towards the pool. "Go ahead and change into your swimsuit, I know you are dying to dive in there. You did good today, go have some fun now"

LESSON: Whether you believe the world is one of abundance or one of scarcity, you are right.

CHAPTER FOUR
Middle Class

How much money do we need to be 'middle class'?" asked Tommy, before he even sat down for his weekly session with the Old Man. "My Mom said that we are still trying to get into the middle class. What does she mean, and how much money do we need to get there?"

The Old Man could tell by Tommy's insistence that this topic was important to him, and his mother also. This was a tricky question with many complex answers, but he knew Tommy did not want or need a dissertation on the definition of middle class, or the textbook definitions of poor or wealthy either. He needed an answer that he could embrace and that would make him feel better about his family's status right now, not at some point in the future.

Helping someone design a better future is only useful to them if you can give them credible hope that they can get to that future. He decided against talking to Tommy about income levels and how the middle class had been shrinking for years now. He would spare him all the details of income inequality and the many factors that contributed to that inequality.

Tommy was clearly in no mood for an academic lecture, he needed a concept that he could hold on to and possibly even share with his mother to help them with their path towards prosperity.

"It is actually quite simple, Tommy," the Old Man began, "as far as money goes, people fall into four basic categories: the poor, the middle class, the wealthy, and the truly prosperous or super wealthy. The main difference between these groups is not dollar amounts of money or income levels, it is the way they think that separates them. The money and income levels simply rise or fall to match those ways of thinking."

"I don't understand" said Tommy quietly.

If Tommy were a little older, the Old Man would teach him about Maslow's hierarchy of needs which explains in detail how a person's current condition dictates what they are focused on and how they cannot move forward until certain needs are met. Instead, he chose a simplified version to teach to Tommy.

"Tommy, if you are really hungry when you get home from school, what is the first thing you do when you get home?" asked the Old Man.

"Look in the fridge for something to eat, of course." came the answer. "Wouldn't it be better for your future to study instead?" the Old Man replied

"Well, yeah, I guess so, but it is hard to think about the future when you are hungry." Tommy wasn't sure what this had to do with his question, but he went along anyway.

The Old Man was pleased that Tommy had grasped the very essence of the lesson so naturally. He explained to Tommy, "Poor people tend to be focused on meeting their most urgent needs, or surviving, so they mainly worry about their money on a weekly basis. They are most concerned with simply surviving one week to the next.

"Middle class people tend to worry more on monthly terms. They usually have enough food, but they are concerned with obligations like mortgage payments, rent, utilities and insurance bills, most of which are paid monthly. Thus, middle class folks tend to have a monthly perspective, sometimes thought of as a 'security' focus. They aren't hungry, but they do not feel secure because they worry about meeting their monthly obligations.

"Once people have gotten past survival and security, they are able to focus on moving towards freedom, which is where the wealthy and prosperous folks dwell. These folks think of things in terms of an annual perspective. They think about increasing their annual income. They devise tax strategies for each year.

"They are not much concerned with monthly bills because they earn enough to pay them without much thought or concern. Their goal is not just having enough to pay their current bills, they are planning ways to accumulate enough wealth to be able to pay all their bills without going to work every day. This would give them the freedom to spend their days as they wish.

This is where most people want to live.

"Most people do not need expensive toys or objects, they simply want to spend as many of their remaining days as they can, doing what they wish, with whom they wish to do them."

Tommy was following along well, but the Old Man had forgotten one category of people, the truly prosperous or super wealthy. These were the people Tommy wanted to know about.

"The truly prosperous and super wealthy spend most of their planning time working on generational plans. They think about how they can preserve their wealth for their children and grandchildren. They are not worried about themselves anymore, they are worried about future generations of their family. They also tend to be the ones who are most able to help other people achieve their own prosperity. They know enough about money and wealth that they share what they know with others, often for free. They want other people to know the same feeling of freedom and prosperity they feel because it makes them feel even better when others do well also.

"Well, I guess that we are middle class after all, because my Mom definitely spends her time worrying about our monthly bills. But, how does someone get to the next level? If you are hungry, how do you NOT worry about it?" Tommy asked.

"The plain truth is Tommy, you have to conquer the survival level before you can move on. The only way I know of to do that is to make yourself think like the folks on the next level. If you are poor, you must get past worrying about this week, and start thinking about this month.

"You have to stop worrying about this week's paycheck and start planning ways to make more money every month and every year. Instead of just trying to work more hours, you have got to think about developing more skills to make more money per hour and not just more hours.

19

"If you are middle class, you must start getting your monthly bills under control, so you can focus more on annual goals and strategies. You must look for ways to reduce or eliminate some costs, so you can start saving to invest. You must set annual savings and investing goals and start working on ways to increase your annual income, and that includes using smart tax strategies to increase how much you keep every year.

"Once you get to this point, the point where you have enough investments to pay your bills whether you work or not, then you must decide if you are satisfied to stay there and kick back and relax or if you want to go to the next step, to become truly prosperous. To do this, you must spend some of the time that you used to spend working, instead looking for investment opportunities as if it were your job. You look for ways to contribute to your community and help other folks take the next step in their journey. You teach your children what you know and encourage them to learn things you do not know. You teach them how to preserve the money you will leave to them and teach them how to enjoy it while still growing it for their kids."

The Old Man knew this was way more than Tommy could retain in one sitting, but he reassured him that they would continue to discuss this as they went forward. Everything he would teach him in the future revolved around this idea of where to focus your attention. The farther you want to go, the farther down the road you must look.

Tommy wasn't certain about everything he just heard, but he was relieved to find out that he and his mother were middle class after all. But now that he heard about the rest of the levels, middle class didn't sound so great after all, but it was a start.

LESSON: Poor people think in weekly terms, middle class people think in monthly terms, rich people think in annual terms, and the truly prosperous think in generational terms.

CHAPTER FIVE
Wishes, Hopes, and Plans

Feeling satisfied that his first few lessons with Tommy had gone well, and that the boy understood what he heard, the Old Man decided to reinforce the concept of an abundant world with the next logical step in the boy's education. Clearly, one must wonder why so many people struggle in the presence of such abundance.

The Old Man knew that even if Tommy couldn't express the sentiment, he would soon be feeling it on a deeper level. He hoped to address it with some further clarification this Saturday.

The boy arrived on time, and knocked before entering, as the Old Man had instructed the previous week. It was these small details that fueled his hope for Tommy. If he could instill in him the ability to remember directions and then follow them, he had a chance at being successful. Success is quite often the predictable result of following a simple plan long enough to achieve results. That was going to be the main point of today's lesson.

After their new ritual of raiding the fridge for a snack for the boy, and preparing a cup of coffee for himself, they settled in the living room to begin. Tommy wasted no time in voicing his skepticism regarding a previous lesson. Rather, he appeared to be voicing his mother's skepticism, but it did not matter. Either way, the Old Man knew that it was coming, and he was prepared for it.

"My mom said there is no such thing as magic and no such thing as free money." The boy was visibly upset and confused. The man who seemed to know a lot about money and the mother he loved and trusted more than anyone in the world were telling him different things.

This was delicate territory for the Old Man to navigate. He had to give Tommy more information without directly contradicting the boy's mother. He could do his best to help the boy, but if he offended his mother or forced Tommy to choose between them, everyone would lose, especially Tommy himself.

"She is right, Tommy, on both counts. Let me explain. I said that building a house on a piece of land was like doubling my money, which was like magic. It might seem like magic on paper because the dollars doubled, but the whole truth is a little more complicated. Are you ready to learn more?"

Tommy was clearly relieved that the Old Man didn't call his mother a liar or say she was wrong, he'd been expecting a fight, but was happy to see that one was not going to happen. He liked the Old Man and wasn't thrilled about confronting him in the first place. He nodded for the Old Man to continue.

"What really happened is that my plan to build a house started a series of events that caused people to work hard and that work became the extra money that just looked like magic if you didn't know better, does that make sense?" he asked.

When the boy hesitated, he explained further. "Because I studied a lot and learned from some truly smart people, I knew that if I bought that piece of land and hired a builder to build a house on it, I could make my money grow and help other people make money too. It was my plan that made it work like it did".

The boy nodded, but he did so without much confidence. The Old Man took a slightly different approach. "Tommy, what would have happened if I just wished for a house to be built on that land?"

Tommy laughed. He knew the answer to this question. "Nothing."

"What would have happened if I had hoped for it to be built?" the Old Man continued. "Nothing." Tommy repeated.

"Okay, then, why did it get built?" the Old Man inquired hopefully.

It took Tommy a second, but he remembered what was said a few minutes ago. "You planned for it!" he said.

"Tommy, my boy, you just learned the biggest secret of all!" the Old Man congratulated the boy.

The Old Man elaborated. "Tommy, the reason so many people never really succeed is that too many of them spend their lives wishing and hoping that something good will happen to them. Good things very rarely happen to people without them planning for them in advance. Tommy, good things do not come to those who wait, good things come to those who plan for good things.

"Wishing and hoping are fine for things that we cannot control, like the weather or whether or not our favorite team wins a game. But if we want things in our lives to get better, we need to stop wishing and hoping and start planning and then doing. Sometimes it is even necessary to adjust or even change the plan, but it is crucial to always have a plan to follow. People without plans often end up somewhere they do not want to be, on the wrong end of someone else's plan."

Tommy asked, "Why don't more people make plans if they are so important?"

The Old Man said, "Most people start off with plans, big ones. The truth is, most plans are not very good when they are first made. Life has too many things that can change quickly and make a mess of our plans. When this happens, many people try for a while, but then give up before they do well. Sometimes, people quit because they don't have enough knowledge about what they are trying to do to be able to adjust."

"Remember the house I built on that piece of land?" the Old Man asked. The boy nodded.

"A lot of people could make that plan, it is really simple, there are houses everywhere. A lot of people make that same plan every day, but they don't end up with a house. Why? Because if they have a problem with getting the money, they don't know what to do. I know a lot of different ways to get the money.

"If they don't know what kind of house would be best on that land, they put the wrong kind and have problems. I know the right kind to build. There are lots of reasons that people fail, even if they make plans, Tommy. That is why it is so important that they learn the stuff I am teaching you now. Schools don't teach kids these things."

He could tell by the look on Tommy's face that he was losing the boy's attention and decided to stop there before the boy's mind wandered off too far.

"Don't worry, Tommy. By the time it is your turn to build a house, you will know everything you need to know and more."

The boy smiled, because he knew the Old Man was telling him the truth and because he could tell by his tone that he was done learning for the day. The weather outside was too miserable to go swimming, but the Old Man had let him bring over his video game console and hook it up to the large flat screen television in the living room.

Tommy knew he had several hours of gaming before his mother came for him, and he wasn't going to let a minute of it go to waste. The Old Man brought his coffee cup to the sink and set it down. He allowed himself a small grin, as he was confident that the boy had the potential to learn what he was teaching and someday, share it with others also.

The Old Man was finally beginning to fully grasp what his own mentor and his own lessons said about generational thinking. It wasn't just about making financial plans with the next generation in mind, it was about helping to equip the next generation to handle the responsibilities and the possibilities of the world they would be inheriting from us.

LESSON: Wishes and hopes are fine for things we cannot control, but prosperity requires a plan.

CHAPTER SIX

Opportunity

This week would only be Tommy's fifth visit with him, but the Old Man could already tell that Tommy was quite bright. He had easily learned the terms and concepts that he taught him so far. He asked lots of questions and was a bit restless, but he clearly was paying closer attention that he had expected.

He also realized, however, that there would soon come a time when his lessons would become tiresome if he couldn't help Tommy experience the real-life results of what he was learning.

Tommy and his mother were still living in a different reality than the one depicted by the Old Man. His stories would start to sound like fairy tales if he was unable to demonstrate the power of the simple concepts he was teaching.

He devised a powerful way to give Tommy an opportunity to use what he was learning to improve his life and help to shape the general attitude of both Tommy, and hopefully, his mother also.

The Old Man knew that unless he could resolve, in Tommy's mind, the conflict between what he was learning and what he was experiencing, his lessons would be useless to Tommy. Real life experience always trumps academic learning if the two do not seem to agree. He briefly spoke with Tommy's skeptical mother who reluctantly agreed to the plan.

Saturday came, and true to form, Tommy was loudly chewing what must have been four pieces of gum at the same time. He plopped down on the couch in his usual spot and got his notebook ready for another afternoon of writing and listening. He had the rest of the pack dangling from his pocket. Tommy always seemed to have a full supply when he came for his lessons.

"What's that?" he asked as he gestured towards the pack hanging from Tommy's front pocket.

"Gum." Tommy answered quietly, leaving out the 'duh' in his head. He knew the Old Man was not a fan of sarcasm.

"Where did you get it?" the Old Man continued. "From a kid at school." Tommy replied.

"Did he give it to you?" the Old Man asked.

"Of course not," came the reply. Tommy was beginning to think the Old Man was making small talk instead of helping him, but he knew better than that. The Old Man liked small talk as much as he liked sarcasm, not at all. Tommy continued, "I bought it from him."

"How much did you pay for that pack of gum?" "Fifty cents." Tommy answered.

"Whoa! Fifty cents! Don't you know that same gum costs twenty-five cents in the grocery store?" the Old Man asked.

"Yeah, but we don't have a grocery store in school," came the defense. "Where did the other boy get the gum?"

"At the store, I guess." Tommy was starting to understand where this was going.

"So, this other boy buys gum at the store for twenty-five cents and sells it to other kids at school for fifty cents. Is that right?" the Old Man summarized. "How many packs does he sell every day?"

"A bunch! Everybody buys it from him, they line up between classes," Tommy was already becoming more interested.

"Why don't you do what he does?" asked the Old Man.

Tommy pondered the idea for a minute, then slumped down a bit again. "Because everybody already buys from him. They won't buy from me."

"You are probably right. Why would they buy from you for the same price as the other guy? But, what if you sold it to them for twenty-five cents, the same price as the store? Then would they buy it from you instead of him?"

"They sure would, but why would I buy it for twenty-five cents and sell it for the same price?"

"What does your Mom's new boyfriend do for a living?" the Old Man asked. He had met the boyfriend and found him to be a nice enough fellow and he already knew the answer.

"He sells stuff to the grocery stores," came the reply.

"What kind of stuff?" the Old Man was clearly going to have to lead the boy right up to it this time, but the lesson was important.

"You know, food, milk, bread, stuff like that." Tommy answered.

"What else?" the Old Man asked patiently. "Visualize the inside of the store, what else is in the store?"

Tommy closed his eyes and imagined the inside of the store he had been in many times. He smiled as he came to his favorite section, the gum and candy section. "Candy and gum!" he exclaimed.

"Bingo!" the Old Man said. He was pleased with his young friend's change in mood. The energy he usually brought in was back, and it was quite pleasant to the Old Man, more so than he would have admitted just a few months ago.

"Tommy, there are several ways businesses make money. There are several different models that, in some form or another, almost all businesses copy.

"One of the most basic models is the wholesale/retail model. This is where stores or entrepreneurs buy goods in bulk at cheaper prices and then sell them individually for slightly higher prices to the actual customers. This is the way most stores make their money. They buy their stuff in large quantities from distributors or manufacturers and then resell them.

"Another model is where someone might buy something large and then divide it into smaller pieces to sell to other people. Land developers sometimes use this model. Selling services instead of products is another common model. Selling services is a good way for a beginner to get started if raising the money to buy stuff is a challenge. The first way is how you are going to start your first business.

"You are going to buy gum and candy wholesale from your mom's boyfriend and sell it at retail prices to your friends at school."

When Tommy's eyes lit up at this statement, the Old Man instructed Tommy to talk to his Mom's boyfriend.

Eager to score brownie points with Tommy's mother, the man agreed to sell Tommy candy and gum at wholesale prices. Impressed with the boy's initiative, he even agreed to advance him the first box of gum. The wholesale price worked out to be twelve and a half cents per pack.

Tommy sold it in school for twenty-five cents and doubled his money on every pack he sold, which was a lot of packs!

Tommy sold as much as he could carry every day before lunch time. He knew he was missing sales and that he needed help. When asked, the Old Man explained to Tommy the concept of commission sales. Tommy had several friends help him sell his gum and candy. He let them keep twenty-five cents out of every dollar's worth of gum and candy that they sold. It was less profit than when he sold stuff personally, but with four friends selling, it added up quickly.

After a full school year of selling gum and candy, the school principal shut down Tommy's business. Too many kids were arriving late for class because they were delayed buying candy from Tommy between classes.

Tommy was disappointed, but he was still encouraged by his success and had made and saved several thousand dollars. This was money that he earned, no one gave it to him, so it felt like much more money than it really was, but it was a substantial sum for a boy his age. He did as he had been taught. He bought a few things he wanted and saved the rest for his next venture.

LESSON: Opportunity never knocks, but it is everywhere and doesn't care how young you are or how old, just how open your eyes are!

CHAPTER SEVEN
Tommy's Mother

Norah, Tommy's mother, waved the Old Man down as he got out of his car carrying groceries. She seemed insistent on getting his attention, so he set the bags down and walked to the fence that separated their yards.

She smiled broadly as he approached "I have to admit that I was skeptical about Tommy selling gum in school, but he sure is excited, and he seems to have made a whole lot of money for a boy his age. If the principal hadn't shut him down, who knows how much he would have made. I can't thank you enough for what you have done for him. His whole attitude towards life is better. Last night, he did his homework without being asked! I can't tell you how big that is for us.

"My boyfriend says Tommy was his biggest candy customer for a while. The stores buy a few boxes each week. Tommy was buying a few boxes every day. We knew it couldn't last forever, but it seems to have been a great lesson for him, heck, even for me. If the kid can learn to start a business and make money, maybe there is hope for me yet."

When she stopped talking long enough to catch her breath, the Old Man said, "No thanks are necessary, Tommy is a good kid and listens well. I am glad to help any way I can. Forgive me for asking, but how are you doing? The new job paying you enough?"

She sighed, "Well, I am making more than I ever did, but I still seem to not have anything left over at the end of the month for us.

The bills eat up every dollar, just like they always have. The more I make, the more they take. Maybe Tommy will strike it rich in time to help his mother out, what do you think?"

"I have no doubt Tommy will end up fine and be able to take care of his mother eventually, but why wait for that to happen? You are a young woman and have plenty of time to plan your own path to prosperity. You and Tommy could work together and get there much faster," the Old Man said.

"That sounds great, but I'm having trouble making ends meet, it's hard to see prosperity from where I am right now," she answered.

The Old Man knew he had to help her. If she continued to struggle without some sort of plan, she would be no help to Tommy and she would even end up sabotaging his efforts, not intentionally, but subtly and without realizing she was doing it. Financial struggles are inherited just as surely as wealth is passed down. Some people leave money as an inheritance. Others leave a legacy of suffering and aimlessness. If Tommy was going to succeed, he would have to bring his mother along with him.

"Tommy tells me you make a mean marinara sauce and your meatballs are world class. Is that right?" he asked her.

She was a little confused by the change of subject, but she really was an excellent cook and was proud that her son was apparently bragging about her skills. "If he says so, it must be true." she replied.

"Tell you what, tomorrow night whip up a batch of your famous meatballs and invite me for dinner. Get all your bills and statements together. After dinner, I'll take a quick peek at what you have going on and see if I can make some suggestions. Does that sound good?" he offered.

She smiled, and he noticed her shoulders relax a bit and her demeanor brighten just a little bit.

It occurred to him that maybe it had been some time since anyone extended her a hand without expecting it to be filled with her hard-earned money.

"Seven o'clock sound good?" She knew enough about the Old Man and his gift for financial matters to jump on the chance to enlist his help with her situation. If anyone could help her, it was likely to be him.

"I will be there." he answered.

He returned to his car to finish unloading his groceries and was surprised to see her follow him to his car and grab a few bags. She followed him inside and placed the bags on the kitchen table. She turned to leave, but she stopped short, turned back towards him, and gave him an unexpected hug and a sincere "thank you" before heading out the front door.

He fought his emotions as he realized it had been a year since anyone hugged him. He felt just a tiny bit of the man that had died with his wife returning for a fleeting moment, and he liked the feeling.

He spent the next few hours reviewing his notes on basic financial matters like insurance, consumer debt and the like. It had been many years since he had given these things a thought. He spent most of his time monitoring things like stock market fluctuations, foreign and emerging markets, and bond yields.

He felt a twinge of shame when he considered how many other people could use his help getting past worrying about basic financial items like insurance and debt. While he had spent a lifetime guarding against becoming greedy with his wealth, had he instead become greedy with his knowledge and wisdom? Tommy was his first real student and he had been quite prosperous by most standards for several decades now.

Thinking back, he remembered how many times his wife had suggested he "go talk" to someone that she knew to be struggling. He had always resisted her with the excuse he didn't want to be nosy, but now he knew that he could have found a way to help if he had sincerely wanted to, and it saddened him to know that his wife must have known the truth. What did she think of him when he refused to help?

At 6:55, he grabbed his calculator, a notebook, and several pens and headed out the front door to visit Tommy and Norah next door. This would be the first time he had been in their home, though they had lived next door for months now.

Tommy opened the door with a huge grin before he even reached the top of the stairs. The boy was clearly excited that the Old Man was coming to his home to help his mother. Since he started making money in school selling gum and candy, the Old Man's status had gone up many notches in the boy's eyes. Now his new hero was going to help his mother and he couldn't be happier.

As promised, Norah's sauce and meatballs were better than any he had ever tasted. This appraisal included his own wife's cooking, but he kept that to himself for now. He also smelled the familiar scent of homemade chocolate chip cookies, a simple treat, but one of his favorites.

After Tommy and his mother cleared the table, she brought out a large file folder overflowing with papers and sheepishly set it down in front of the Old Man. When he didn't run away, she looked relieved, but still a bit nervous. Having financial difficulties can be embarrassing, but only by shining light on the problems can they be solved. She was more than ready for some solutions, problems-she had plenty of those.

The Old Man sorted for a moment and picked out a bank statement from the previous month. He knew this would give him a good snapshot of where her money was going each month. He saw the biggest expense was her rent payment, which was not unusual. The next biggest item he noticed was a $200 payment to an insurance company. He inquired as to what type of insurance the premium was for. She told him it was a life insurance policy she bought in case something happened to her. "How much coverage does this policy give you for this premium?", he asked.

"I believe it is around $100,000." she answered.

That amount of coverage for that much premium seemed a bit off to him. "Can you locate this actual policy for me?" he asked.

She said she could and left to go into her bedroom. She returned in just a few minutes and handed him the policy. As he suspected, she had purchased an expensive cash-value or whole- life policy.

"How long ago did you buy this policy?" he asked.

"About two years ago. I wanted to do it sooner, but I couldn't afford to." she answered.

"Let me guess, when you bought this policy, they told you it would build up some cash value that you could access later if you needed it, does that sound right?" he asked.

"Yes, and they said I could keep it forever as long as I paid the premiums."

"After two years of paying premiums, how much cash value would you guess is built up in this policy so far?" asked the Old Man.

"A fair bit, I guess. Maybe a few thousand?" she offered, uncertain because she hadn't checked.

"They have charts in these policies that show how much you accumulate year after year.

Look at this chart here. At two years in, you have exactly zero dollars. Does that surprise you?" he asked.

He could see her becoming visibly angry and let her experience the emotion for a minute. It was important to let that emotion arise and settle before he offered her a better idea.

"This will be the first thing we address for two reasons. There is another type of life insurance that is called term insurance. It is insurance only, it has no investment function at all. It is pure insurance and lasts for a limited period, or term. Generally, you buy a policy whose term lasts for as long as you expect to have someone dependent on your income to survive. Does that make sense?" She nodded, still looking a little angry.

"The reason that is important is because it is only insurance, so it costs much less to buy. Since it costs so much less, you can afford to buy the right amount of insurance to fulfill its purpose. If I am correct, this policy would replace your current income for around two years. Tommy is ten now and this would provide for him until he was twelve. With a term policy, you could buy enough coverage to last him until adulthood if something happened to you.

"The second reason this is so important is that the difference in premium is money back in your pocket. This is money we can now use to partially fund your retirement account. We will replace the 'investment' inside this old policy with an actual investment that you control. It would be hard to do worse than zero dollars after two years, wouldn't it?"

Norah's anger had subsided somewhat, and she was anxious to talk to the agent who had sold her the policy and cancel it. The Old Man took a business card from his wallet and handed it to her.

"Call this woman. She specializes in replacing these types of policies. Do not cancel your old policy until you have a new policy firmly in place. You never want to be uninsured. Bad insurance is better than no insurance at all. The process is simple. Once you make this change, we will work on the next step when we know how much money this will save you. Does that sound smart?"

She agreed to call his agent the next day to start the change right away. She picked up the rest of her pile and brought the plate of cookies to the table.

LESSON: Prepare for the worst, plan for the best!

CHAPTER EIGHT
Two Messengers

A few days after the Old Man had visited with Norah and Tommy and helped her with her life insurance, she came by his house to update him on her progress. "Well, I talked to the agent you recommended, and by her estimate, I will save around $100 per month and have a lot more coverage for my money. Thank you for your advice. I think this is a good start. What do I do next?" she asked.

"If you are free this evening, I can come by and share my 'two messengers' strategy with you, I think it will be helpful," he offered.

"Seven o'clock sound good? I'm making pork chops tonight and I have plenty for three people." she answered.

"I will be there." said the Old Man.

He arrived right at seven and he found Norah's pork chops to be as tasty as her meatballs and marinara. Once dinner was finished, he wasted little time getting down to talking about the next step in her journey.

"Ok, now we essentially have one hundred dollars per month to work with, is that right?" When she nodded, he went on. "The first thing we need to think about after making sure Tommy is taken care of should something happen to you, is we need to make plans for the possibility that nothing bad will happen to you. We need to make sure senior citizen Norah has the money she needs to enjoy her golden years in style. The strategy I am going to suggest to you is what I call the two messengers strategy.

"When our country was first founded, we had many wars and conflicts. It was often necessary for generals and other leaders to send messages to their superiors or fellow generals to make plans for attacks and defenses, things like that. Since they didn't have phones or fax machines, they sent runners. They groomed the fastest runners to carry messages through tough terrain and often past enemy forces to whomever they needed to convey the information.

"Often, many lives depended on these messages reaching their destination. If a messenger was killed or captured, many lives could be lost. To increase the chances of an important message getting through, they usually sent two messengers by different routes, carrying the same message. That way, if one failed to get through, the other would continue and make the delivery.

"In terms of your financial future, we are going to send at least two different messengers into the future with a message for senior citizen Norah. We are going to send one the slow and steady way and then we are going to work on a speedier way also. Does that make sense to you?"

Norah was engaged and said, "Kind of a Plan A and Plan B situation?"

"Yes, but we are planning for both messengers to get through, which will make senior citizen Norah extra happy and secure." he answered.

"The first messenger we are going to send into the future is a retirement plan. Do you have one available to you at work?" he asked.

"No, we have nothing like that where I work, but the hourly pay is pretty good," she answered.

"Ok, then we need to look into what is called a Roth IRA for you. A Roth IRA is a plan that you fund with after tax dollars, like the money you saved on your insurance. Since you already paid taxes on that money, it can grow inside your Roth tax-free, and when you take the money out in retirement, it is still tax-free. With me so far?" he asked.

"Yes, but I don't know anything about picking stocks or the market at all. How do I know what to invest in?" she asked, seeming a bit concerned.

"That is fine for this particular messenger. Many professionals spend their entire lives trying to pick the right stocks at the right time. They have all the computers, programs, charts and information you could imagine. Guess what? Over any extended period almost none of them do better than the market in general. Most do worse than the market.

"The stock market has averaged 8-10 percent gain per year for decades now. This doesn't mean it gains that much every year consistently. As a matter of fact, it is wildly inconsistent from one year to the next. But over any long period of time, it generally moves up on average 8-10 percent per year. At 8 percent, your money will double every nine years.

"If you put in one thousand dollars now, and the markets average 8 percent, in nine years, that one thousand will be two thousand. Nine years later, four thousand, and so forth. This is called the Rule of 72. If you take the number 72 and divide it by your rate of gain, the result is the number of years it takes one dollar to turn into two dollars.

"Are you still with me?" he asked.

"So far so good, but if no one is very good at picking stocks, how am I supposed to get that average return?" she asked.

"Actually, that answer is fairly simple. You buy the whole market. Whatever the market does, you go along with it. Obviously, you cannot buy the whole market with a hundred bucks a month. However, there are companies that do have enough money to do just that.

"They take your money and add it to the money of thousands or even millions of other folks and use that money to buy some of every company in the market. They call these index funds. They have different ones for different markets, but they all work similarly. Since the managers do not have to make a lot of decisions, the costs are low, which helps you keep more of what you make for yourself.

"Since it will be a long while before you need this money, you have time to ride out the ups and downs of the markets without worrying too much. When you get closer to retirement, we will adjust your holdings into more conservative things, but for now, we will be somewhat aggressive.

"The catch is that this approach will take decades to accumulate enough money for you to retire on and it is still dependent on markets that can be volatile sometimes.

"Once we have this messenger set up for you, we will look at the rest of your stuff and discuss ways to create another messenger. This one will be a bit faster and may get you to your retirement goals much sooner than the first messenger. Retirement is not an age, it is a number. Once you have enough money accumulated that the interest it generates can pay your expenses, you are technically free. You can decide to keep working or not. You can work less, or work on something you like. You can travel or start a business. The important thing is that you will be able to decide for yourself how you want to spend your days.

"You might reach that amount in a few years, ten years, or never. Sadly, most folks never fully experience true financial freedom because they only send one messenger or even fail to send any. That is a tragedy in my opinion."

Figuring that they had covered enough ground for one night, the Old Man gathered his things and prepared to leave. Norah reached across the table and touched his hand. "Thank you again for doing this. I know we haven't really started much yet, but I already feel some hope, and it has been a while since that has happened."

The Old Man was touched by her gratitude, but it also amplified the lingering guilt he felt when he thought of how many other people needed exactly this type of help and weren't getting it.

How many people are out there feeling hopeless when a few hours of planning and education could change their outlook completely? This was the question that haunted him every night and every day. If he were younger and had it to do over again, he definitely would have listened to his wife more and just talked to those he knew needed his help.

LESSON: Retirement is not an age, it is a number. When you have the assets that produce enough income, you are free!

CHAPTER NINE
Financial Education

The Old Man wanted to change the setting for his next session with Norah. He invited Norah and Tommy to eat dinner with him at Nessa's Steakhouse, the fanciest restaurant in their town. When she objected over the cost, he made it clear that he was treating them, and she reluctantly agreed. He stressed to her that even though this place was a bit pricey, the atmosphere was casual.

When they arrived, it was obvious that the Old Man had been here before. The manager greeted him warmly and asked if he wanted his usual table. The Old Man nodded and asked the manager about his wife and children. When they sat down, the waiter also greeted them with a huge smile and warm handshake.

As they read the menus, Norah and Tommy were a bit taken aback by the prices on the right side of the menu. Each item was several times more expensive than the restaurant they usually frequented. The Old Man set them at ease, "Please do not be shy, order whatever looks good. Everything here is excellent. Isn't that right, Tony?" he looked towards the waiter.

"Yes, sir! Our chefs are the best around, I guarantee you will not be disappointed with anything you order," came the reply.

They ordered some appetizers and drinks, and Tony hurried away to place their order and get their drinks.

As he vanished, the Old Man told Tommy and Norah to look around at some of the other patrons. He asked them to notice how perfectly normal and average they all looked. He pointed out several groups of people as he waved to them. He apparently knew most of the other customers. He told them who some of these people were. Some were local business owners, and some were local politicians.

Most of them were regulars at this restaurant, as was the Old Man. He made it a point to explain how average these people all were except for one distinction: They were all prosperous to a greater or lesser degree. None of them were worried about the numbers on the right-hand side of the menu.

The Old Man wanted Tommy and Norah to see that the wealthy and prosperous were just people like them. They were not special in any other way but one. They understood how money works, better than most people.

"Norah, if I am correct, you are an RN, a registered nurse. Is that right?" asked the Old Man.

"Yes, I am," she replied proudly. She had worked hard and studied extensively to achieve her current designation.

"Before you were an RN, what was your designation?"

"Before I became an RN, I was an LPN, a licensed practical nurse, and before that, I was a CNA, a certified nurse's assistant."

"Once again, if I am correct, each level required more education and more studying, but came with a significant pay raise, is that accurate?" the Old Man continued.

Norah was a little confused by the questions, but she knew there was a point to them. "Yes, of course. The more education you get, the more you know and the more you get paid. Pretty fair, actually."

"Okay, that right there is the main reason some people become prosperous and wealthy, but most folks struggle throughout their entire lives."

"Becoming wealthy is more a result of financial education than vocational education. What you have done so well is to increase your vocational education level and value. That is a great start. The problem is that you left your financial education at the high school level, at best. You learned how to make a paycheck and pay some bills, and that is where you stopped learning about money.

"I am not criticizing you, that is what most people do. They advance their technical job skills but fail to advance their education regarding what to do with the money they make. You do not become prosperous by what you make at work, you become prosperous by what you do with the money you make at work. No paycheck will ever be large enough if you don't have a plan for it after you receive it."

The Old Man paused and leaned back as Tony placed his appetizer in front of him. Tommy and Norah smiled as their food arrived, the portions were generous, and the plates were beautifully presented. Norah smiled at her plate, then looked across at the Old Man. She looked around the restaurant and started to absorb what he was telling her.

"The only difference between you and these other folks is a financial education. I guarantee that you know more about anatomy and physiology than anyone else here. If someone had a medical issue right now, you would likely be the most valuable person in this restaurant immediately. Now, what you need to do if you want to achieve some level of financial freedom is apply some of your extensive study skills towards a new subject. We must take your high school diploma level financial education and elevate it to a college graduate level. We need you to become an RN of money."

Norah knew he was right. It was obvious now that he pointed it out to her. The idea of learning a whole new subject was a bit intimidating, but she saw now that there was no other way forward. There would be no lottery winnings, there was no inheritance coming. Tommy would likely do well with the Old Man's teaching, but it would be a while before he was old enough to really help her. If she wanted to be free, education was clearly the only way.

"Okay, I believe you. I want to know more about money, but I don't think there are any classes I can take. How do I get started?" she asked.

"Well, fortunately for all of us, many of the world's wealthiest people like to brag a bit.

Many of them have written multiple books describing, with great details, exactly how they made their money. They teach about methods and strategies, but even more importantly, they teach about the mindsets, attitudes, and philosophies that guide them every day. That is actually the more important factor."

"Books I can handle. College involved lots of books," she said.

"Lucky for you, these books are generally less dry than textbooks. Some are fascinating to read. Even luckier for you, I have read almost all of them over the years. I have an extensive library at home and I can help you choose which books to read and in what order will make sense. If you are willing, I will help you and Tommy to undertake an adventure into a whole new world, a world where you can eat wherever you like whenever you like." He gestured towards the open restaurant and the people eating there.

Their steaks arrived. Tony asked them all to cut into their steaks to make sure they were prepared properly. The Old Man cut into his filet mignon and looked inside. It was a perfect medium rare, just as he ordered. Norah and Tommy followed his lead and pronounced them perfect. Tony smiled broadly and left them to enjoy their meals.

LESSON: It is not your vocational education that will make you prosperous, it is only your financial education that can do that.

CHAPTER TEN
The Lottery Loser

The Old Man liked to use the time between waking up on Saturday mornings and when Tommy arrived to catch up on the news. He would turn on his flat screen, prepare a large cup of coffee and flip through the local news channels, and if he had time, the national news channels.

This morning, he was watching a local news reporter interview a man who was visibly upset. The banner running across the bottom of the screen read "Lottery winner says winning ruined his life."

The reporter was asking the guy exactly how he ended up broke and in debt after winning ten million dollars just three years ago, when Tommy came in. He instantly recognized the man's face. "Yeah, we saw that guy on the news last night too. He was crying about how the lottery ruined his life! What a loser he is!" Tommy said.

The Old Man saw an opportunity to teach Tommy an important lesson about life and about money at the same time. "Why do you call him a loser, Tommy?" inquired the Old Man.

"Because he LOST ten million bucks in three years! What else should I call him?" came the answer.

"What do you think happens to most of the people who win lotteries or inherit a lot of money suddenly, Tommy?"

"I bet they live like kings forever." Tommy replied.

"Sadly Tommy, many, if not most, of them end up more broke than before they got the money."

The Old Man knew Tommy would have trouble believing him because the "get rich quick" fantasy was so prevalent in our culture. So many people truly believe that a sudden windfall would change their lives forever. They are often correct about the change, but rarely about the direction of the change.

"Tommy, did you know that a large percentage of Americans consider winning the lottery to be their best hope for a secure and happy retirement? The saddest part about that idea is that not only are the chances of winning miniscule in the first place, but most of those who do win experience neither comfort nor security for very long after winning."

It was vital to the education of Tommy that the Old Man disabuse Tommy of the notion that sudden riches are a viable path to wealth and prosperity. He had seen far too many people end up miserable because they never got past the harmful "get rich quick" mentality. He had to teach Tommy the reality about unearned money.

"Tommy, why do you think this guy lost all his money?" the Old Man quizzed. Tommy replied quickly, "Because he is stupid, that's why!"

"But this guy was a professor of literature. He had several advanced degrees. His intelligence level is quite high. No, Tommy he wasn't stupid by any measure," came the reply.

"Then he really must have had some bad luck," Tommy guessed.

"Perhaps, but too many people just like him lose their money also, they can't all be unlucky," the Old Man countered.

"I give up, then. If he isn't dumb and he doesn't have bad luck, how the heck did he lose ten million dollars in three years?" Tommy was done guessing and ready to solve the mystery.

The Old Man said, "There are three main reasons that people are generally unable to hold onto windfalls. The first problem is they don't have a financial education. The professor had an extensive education and was highly intelligent, but the world of money has its own vocabulary and its own history and its own rules.

"Many folks know the rudimentary terms like interest and debt and taxes, but they usually have the wrong perspective on even these basic terms. The English professor was as lost handling money as a first-time foreign visitor would have in an English class without being able to speak a word of English. In financial terms, the professor was illiterate.

"The second problem with unexpected and sudden wealth is that the money changes the person's exterior reality before their interior reality can catch up. In other words, they have the bank account of a rich person overnight, but still the self-image of a poor one. This creates a conflict that is disconcerting to them.

"When a person's wealth grows over time due to their own growth and efforts, the interior reality grows as their prosperity grows, so there is no conflict. With sudden wealth, there is a feeling that the money doesn't truly belong to them, and in a sense, it does not belong to them. Their conscience knows that they did not earn the money.

"Their conscience is unable to reconcile the money with the efforts expended. It feels like stolen money, and the consciences of good people cannot tolerate that feeling for very long. Their sub-conscious minds begin immediately to restore balance between their bank accounts and their own efforts to earn money. This means that the sub-conscious works to either justify the money as earned or rid itself of the money, thus resolving the conflict.

"The third problem is that when a huge pile of money changes hands so publicly, it tends to draw attention. People all around suddenly turn their attention to the pile of treasure. People with slightly more knowledge about money decide to help educate the 'winner', for a fee, of course. Some are well meaning, but many are not.

"Many know it is likely that the person receiving sudden wealth is overwhelmed and open to accepting help. Many would take advantage of another's vulnerability, and as terrible as that may be, it happens quite often. Other people who know of the winnings cannot help but be jealous. Some feel justified in asking or demanding a share because they feel like the winner doesn't need all that money for themselves.

"Because of the first two reasons, lottery winners and other recipients of unearned piles of money are hugely susceptible to these kinds of people. They don't know what to do with the money and they don't feel like they deserve it, and that makes them easy targets. Winning a huge sum of money that everyone knows about puts a target on a person's back, and a big one at that. Very few can withstand the attention and soon miss their old simple life. Soon enough, they have it back."

"Wow, I never thought about all that. Now, winning the lottery doesn't sound so great, does it?" Tommy surmised.

"Don't be sad, Tommy. The things I am going to teach you will lead you to much greater prosperity than any lottery, and the best part about it is, you get to keep this money, because you will earn it, you will understand the language of money, and you will know how to protect it"

"What should a person do if they win the lottery, then?" asked Tommy.

"The best idea is to avoid the lottery in the first place. There are much better ways to invest small amounts of money, and it would take a whole book to tell them all the things someone should do if they win the lottery. All I will tell you is the first thing I would do is hire a very good lawyer even before I picked up my check," answered the Old Man.

LESSON: Get the idea of easy money out of your head, you wouldn't get to keep it anyway.

CHAPTER ELEVEN
Passive and Active Income

Talking about the professor who lost ten million dollars in lottery winnings in just three years was a good start in discussing what happens when people do not know enough about money and how it works to keep it, even if it falls in their laps. Tommy had even had a taste of making money himself with his gum and candy business. The Old Man certainly had Tommy's attention now.

It was time for him to start learning the language of money, or more accurately, the language of prosperity. Tommy was getting a handle on the idea of working for money, as most people do. Now it was time to introduce him to the concept of not working for money, a concept that most people grasp on an intellectual level, yet never embrace on a practical level. It was time to teach Tommy the difference between active and passive income.

The Old Man found that people learned new ideas and concepts better when they are tied to lessons they have already learned or to life experiences they had in the past.

"Tommy, do you remember when you sold gum and candy in school?" asked the Old Man.

Tommy smiled broadly. That was his first venture into the business world and it had been a booming success. He still had an impressive pile of money in the bank from that idea. The school principal had ended his thriving business prematurely, but Tommy had it long enough to experience the thrill of business success and the feel of well-deserved money in his pockets. "Yep, I sure do!"

"Today, we are going to talk a bit about the difference between when you sold the gum yourself and when the other kids sold it for you, would that be okay?" asked the Old Man.

Tommy was a bit confused, as he hadn't given any thought to the distinction before now, but if his mentor thought it was important, so did he. "Sure, why not?" he agreed.

"Okay, Tommy. When you were selling the gum in school with the other kids helping, what you really had was two different streams of income. You were making money in two different ways. You were making money from the gum and candy you sold yourself, and you made some money when the other kids sold it for you. With me so far?"

When Tommy nodded, he went on.

"Let's say, one day, you were sick and couldn't go to school. How much gum would you sell yourself that day?" he asked.

Tommy looked at the Old Man sideways, and answered "None, of course."

"Exactly, but how much could the other kids sell while you were home sick?" he continued. "Probably a lot, they would get my customers plus their own." Tommy replied.

"Tommy, you just learned the key to prosperity!"

The Old Man talked to Tommy about the fragility of earned income and the benefits of passive income. "You can only make active, or earned, income for as long as you are healthy and young enough to do so. At some point, we all get older and less healthy, and working becomes more and more difficult, but our expenses continue to be healthy. The way we pay for our things when we can't work is through passive income sources."

"Sadly," he explained, "many people are so focused on how much candy they can sell, they never establish ways for others to sell candy for them also. When they get too tired or sick to keep selling, they end up in a bind. Passive income often takes time to develop. It is not something that you can necessarily turn on as soon as you need it."

Besides the obvious problems with active income, the Old Man taught Tommy about the reality of earned income. He used the gum business once again as an example.

"Tommy, what was the most packs of gum that you sold in a day, personally?" asked the Old Man.

"Probably about fifty packs," he said proudly.

"That same day, about how many packs did your helpers sell, between the four of them?"

Tommy had to think for a minute, as he hadn't really kept accounting records of his fledgling business. "Probably over a hundred together, maybe a hundred and fifty," he said, starting to see where the Old Man was going.

"How many more packs could you sell in a day than that, just you?" he continued. "Not many, I was late for class that day twice." Tommy answered.

"What if you had eight helpers instead of just four? What if you had kids in other schools selling for you as well? Then how many packs a day could you sell?" the Old Man liked how wide the boy's eyes got as he began to grasp the power of passive income.

"Thousands!" Tommy exclaimed.

The Old Man felt confident that he had planted the right seeds in Tommy's young mind. He could see the power of passive income not just as an alternative to protect him when he was unable to sell himself, but also a way to multiply his efforts, and the Old Man knew that multiplying one's efforts is fundamental to achieving some measure of wealth and prosperity.

No one becomes wealthy alone, it is a long journey, and long journeys are best undertaken with groups of like-minded people.

Tommy was excited by this idea, but he had a question, "How can adults make passive income? My mom sure could use some extra money."

The Old Man was reluctant to get too far into the next few lessons right now, but he sensed that this was a good opportunity to share some ideas with the boy that applied to his life now and would give him hope not just for the distant future, but for his and his mother's life right now.

"Tommy, how about the idea of your family starting a small business venture, part time for now, that might bring in a few extra dollars that you and your mom could use for bigger investments, more passive ones?"

He talked to Tommy about his mother's skills and what types of things Tommy himself could do that people would pay for. He told Tommy about some of the things he did as a kid to make and save money. He talked about cutting grass, raking leaves, cleaning out garages and cleaning up yards. He explained about using what he had, youth and energy, to help other people who had less youth and less energy, but more money to pay him for his.

He told Tommy about the newspaper routes he had as a kid, although that wasn't something that kids still did. He told him about selling firewood in the winters. He and a friend made "odd job" business cards in junior high shop class and distributed them around their neighborhood.

He explained that these ideas were not passive income ideas, but that they could help Tommy and his mother accumulate some money for investing in bigger ideas, including passive income ideas that could really grow into something larger and more exciting for them as a family.

"Your mother has a lot of valuable skills, we just need to get her thinking about ways to use those skills outside of her job, and maybe even use them to start a business of her own," the Old Man said.

LESSON: Active income requires your presence; passive income does not.

CHAPTER TWELVE
Stocks and Bonds

The Old Man and Tommy had discussed the difference between active and passive income last week. The Old Man had used Tommy's gum and candy business to illustrate the difference between when Tommy himself sold gum and candy and when others sold it for him. He had explained that when he sold it himself, it was active income and when others sold it, and he made money from their efforts, it was passive income.

In other words, that money came in, whether Tommy worked or not. While this was accurate, he felt it needed some more detailed explanation. Technically speaking, when the others sold the candy, it wasn't 100 percent passive because Tommy still provided them with the supplies and collected the money.

This income was still better than active income for a few obvious reasons, it could continue if he wasn't physically present, and it could be duplicated and multiplied for a more powerful effect. This week, he wanted to talk to Tommy about a more common way that many people developed passive income, and that is through investing in businesses started and run by other people.

A way for people to generate income without needing to be present for the daily activities of the business or having to make decisions about the business itself. The way most Americans do this is through the stock market and publicly traded stocks and bonds.

Most of us invest in this market either directly through our own trading accounts or retirement plans we have through our jobs or businesses.

While most adults understand what stocks and bonds are, many don't learn about investing in them until they are much older. By then they have established many other bad habits and ideas, like spending on things they want first and investing last. These habits keep them from pursuing investments in the markets at a younger age, when doing so would have a powerful compounding effect, which is when the money we make starts to make its own money. This could have multiplied their wealth, if they had become interested and began participating in the markets at an earlier time.

The Old Man was determined that the boy would have some basic understanding of the stock market at a young age. Even if he was too young now to have his own trading account, he would have plenty of time to do further study. That way, when the time came, he would not be scared and could make good decisions about what he was buying and selling. Once again, he chose to use the boy's firsthand experience with his first business venture to illustrate the basic concepts of stocks and bonds.

"Tommy, remember when you started the gum and candy business, your Mom's boyfriend was kind enough to help you out by advancing you those first boxes of gum?" the Old Man asked.

"Yeah, I remember." Tommy said with a grin. "I think my Mom made him do it, but it helped a lot."

"What would you have done if he hadn't offered to help you like that, how would you have started your business without his help?" inquired the Old Man.

Tommy pondered for a minute and said," I guess I would have needed someone else to help me."

"Yes, Tommy, and that is how most business get started. Often, one person has a great idea but no money. They usually must find someone else with money to help them get their business started. But why would they do that? Why would someone help another person, maybe a stranger, start a business? Why would they risk their own money on someone else's idea, knowing it might not work?" The Old

Man was confident that Tommy instinctively knew the answer, he just needed a moment to think it through.

"Because they want to make money from the idea, too." Tommy answered. "Congratulations, Tommy, you just explained the stock market!" said the Old Man.

"Tommy, the stock market is a place where people can sell pieces of their ideas or businesses to other people who want to invest in those ideas and companies. Most of the big companies you know, like the big restaurants that have locations all over, the big computer companies, the big stores, are usually not owned by one person.

"They are usually owned by thousands, or even millions of people. These companies are divided up into small pieces called 'shares' and people can buy shares of companies they like or companies they think will make a lot of money.

"When people buy shares of a company, they expect that company to do well and make a lot of money. If they are right, the value of that share goes up. They can sell it and make a profit, or they can keep it if they think it will be worth more in the future. Some companies even share some of the money they make directly with the people who own the shares. These are called dividends, and they are an important source of passive income for many people who can't or don't want to work anymore.

"If I had helped you to start your business, Tommy, there are two ways I could have done it. I could have bought the candy for you to get started and asked you to share ownership of the business and the profits with me in exchange for my help. If you did well, we would have both made a lot of money. But, if you did badly, I would have lost the money I invested.

"However, there is another way I could have helped you get started. I could have just loaned you the money to get started, and you would have paid me back when you made money, you would have paid me back what I loaned you, plus a little extra as a reward for helping you. That little extra is called interest. We would have decided an amount ahead of time.

"You would have had to pay that money back even if you did badly, but if you did really well, you would still only pay back what we agreed. Got it?"

Tommy said he understood, but the Old Man wanted to make sure, so he elaborated. "These big companies sometimes need money to get started or even to expand. If they sell people shares, they are selling them part of the company, called stock. If they borrow the money instead, they are selling bonds, and bonds are promises to repay a loan, to folks who lend them the money.

"The basic difference between stocks and bonds is that when you buy stock, you are buying a piece of that company, and when you buy bonds, you are loaning that company money. Stocks traditionally make more money in the long run, but they carry more risk. Bonds are generally safer, depending on the company, but they tend to pay less because they are less risky.

Whether you buy bonds or stocks depends on many factors, it is just important to know what you are buying, a piece of the company called equity, or just loaning them money called debt.

The stock market is primarily comprised of debt and equity markets. Owning vs. Loaning.

Norah usually came to the door to walk Tommy home when she finished her Saturday shifts, but today she asked to come inside to visit with the Old Man for a minute before heading home.

"Well, I have been thinking about what you were telling me about starting a business using the skills I already have, and I have an idea I want to run by you for your opinion." She said.

"Excellent! I am very pleased to hear that." Replied the Old Man.

"I was thinking about my patients and what they need. I was trying to think of how I could best serve them with the skills and knowledge I have. It occurred to me that one of the biggest problems for my patients, especially the older ones was not that they didn't receive excellent care once they got to their doctor's office.

"The biggest problem I have observed is getting them to the offices to receive that care. Many of our elderly patients no longer drive and many do not have close family members to help them. A lot of appointments are delayed or missed because of transportation issues.

"My business idea is to start a medical transportation service here in town. I will get a specially equipped van with a lift and wheelchair access. I can get referrals from the doctors and nurses I know. I have already researched what similar services in other areas charge for their service, and I believe I can make a good profit and help a lot of people while doing so."

The Old Man was impressed, and he smiled broadly. "That is an excellent idea, and it sounds perfect for you. My suggestion for moving forward is to check with the state to find out what type of licenses you will need. Talk to a business lawyer to talk about what type of entity to create for your company. After you get that information, we can talk about what funding you will need to get started.

"I am very proud of you for doing this. Many folks never make this move and they live lesser lives because of it. Your boldness will be greatly rewarded, both in financial terms and in terms of how this little guy here sees you." He gestured towards Tommy, who had been watching this whole conversation with his full attention. Tommy sensed that this was an important time for him and his mother.

LESSON: Stocks are tiny pieces of a company and bonds are promises to repay a loan.

CHAPTER THIRTEEN
Dinner Before Dessert

By now, Tommy and Norah were starting to feel hopeful about their prospects for the future. They were no longer afraid of being poor their whole lives. The Old Man had done well in showing them how abundant the world truly was. He had convinced them that creating and building wealth were not very complicated. Tommy had already made some money on his own, he understood the basic ways people invested in businesses, and understood the importance of passive income and Norah had a solid plan to start her first business.

Knowing all this was great for Tommy, but he was still struggling with one question that seemed to discredit all that he had learned so far. He was a kid, and he was learning all these things about money. Surely, all or at least most, adults already knew these things too, and probably knew a lot more than he knew.

If adults knew these concepts, and they all worked and made money, why were so many adults always complaining about money? If they were wealthy, why complain? Even if they weren't wealthy yet, but were on their way, why would they complain?

Tommy was certain he was missing a piece of the puzzle, and maybe even a large piece. As was their protocol, Tommy knew the quickest way to an answer was a question. "Hey, I have a question. Why are so many adults poor if they know all these things you are teaching me? Does this stuff really work, or not?"

The Old Man was happy to see that Tommy was thinking outside the confines of their actual lessons. Intellectual curiosity was one of the biggest factors that determined how far a person could go in terms of attaining wealth. The fact that he questioned everything he was taught was very healthy indeed. Some teachers do not like having their students question what they are taught, but the best ones welcome it and even appreciate it. Students don't question lessons if they aren't interested in the subject.

"Well, Tommy, that is an excellent question. There are two big reasons most adults never achieve the wealth they deserve. It is true that most adults, to some degree, know most of what I have taught you so far. We have been discussing basic stuff up to this point.

"However, there are some adults who never had anyone teach them what they need to know, and they never tried to find out on their own. There are lots of reasons for that, but what I think you are really curious about is the other group of adults, the ones who do know the ideas I have been teaching you, but still never get wealthy, is that right?"

Tommy nodded. The Old Man had been expecting this question, so he had come up with a way of explaining the problem in a way that a ten-year old boy could relate to it.

"Tommy, when you and your Mom had dinner last night, did you have dessert afterwards?" asked the Old Man.

Tommy smiled as he remembered the chocolate chip cookies his Mom had made for them. "Yep, she made cookies."

"Did you eat the cookies first? I bet they smelled great sitting there," continued the Old Man.

Tommy's smile disappeared. "No, I had to eat ALL of my dinner first."

"There is a reason for that Tommy, and I know for a fact that your mother has explained it to you many times. The reason you eat your dinner first is because the vitamins and minerals your body needs are in the dinner, not in the dessert. If you eat the dessert first, you won't eat the dinner after, and you won't get the nutrition you need from the dinner." He continued, "What will you do when you become an adult, and you have no one to make you eat your dinner first, Tommy?"

Tommy's smile returned. "I am going to eat my dessert first!"

The Old Man frowned and said, "Yeah, that's what most adults do, Tommy, and that is the answer to your question. The reason most adults end up broke and never become wealthy is they eat their dessert first, just like you want to."

The Old Man explained to Tommy, "Saving and investing money from your paycheck represents eating your dinner. Saving and investing is the part of your personal finances that is good for you and keeps your financial body healthy and strong. Spending the rest of your check on things you like represents eating dessert, that is the part that is fun, but not going to make you healthy, or wealthy, for that matter.

"What most adults do," he continued, "is they get their paycheck, they pay for all the essentials like food and shelter, then they buy the things they like, they go out to eat, they entertain themselves and their friends.

"They pay for what they need, then they buy what they want, and only then, do they consider investing what they have left. They only invest after they buy everything they want first, and the obvious problem with that is there is always something else they want. There is no end to what people can buy today. There are so many new gadgets being produced every day, there is no way anyone could make enough money to keep up. Guess how much is 'left over' for investing after they buy everything they want, Tommy?"

The boy was sitting quietly, as he realized his intention to eat dessert first was not the right answer! "None." came the answer.

"Right, Tommy. There is never anything left over for investing because there are just too many things people want to buy and do. And you can probably guess what happens when they make more money, huh? They buy more stuff or more expensive stuff. If they make a lot more money, they buy more expensive food and shelter also. No matter how much people make, it will never, ever, be enough if they eat dessert first. Can you guess what the solution is yet, Tommy?"

"Yeah, eat your dinner first," he said glumly.

"Bingo! There is hope for you yet!" replied the Old Man.

"If people eat their dinner first, by investing a percentage of their checks before spending the rest, they would be much more likely to end up wealthy. They would still need to learn a lot of things about money, but having money set aside for investing would be a huge first step. After they set aside some money from their paychecks for investing, they could enjoy some dessert with less guilt and a lot more confidence.

"There is also a weird side effect of handling your money this way. Once a person starts accumulating money for investing and they see that money starting to become a sizable chunk of money, they start to lose their appetite for dessert. They begin to feel the power that comes from having money in the bank. The growing pile of money becomes a growing pile of confidence and freedom. It becomes as addictive as spending money, even more so once they experience their first investing gains, even if it is a modest gain. The first dollars of dividend payments, even if tiny, feel like "won" money.

"A dollar made through investing feels like a hundred dollars made through working. There may not be a scientific basis for this feeling, but it is very real indeed. The trick is to make this a habit. You MUST learn to take a percentage of your paycheck and keep it for yourself. Ten percent is an ideal start, but even a one percent or five percent start will suffice. Once you start, even with a tiny amount, the process will snowball as you experience the effects of a growing account where there was not one previously.

"At ten percent, you would have more than a month's pay saved at the end of the first year, how empowering would that be? How much less stressful would everyday life be with a month's pay set aside? How about two months' worth? Even with no gains, even with the money in a bank savings account, it would feel amazing for someone who never had any money saved to have several months' salary in a bank account.

"Your subconscious mind will notice this good feeling and help you to find ways to enhance and increase this feeling. You will find yourself stalling before buying something you don't really need. Your brain will start to weigh whether or not you would enjoy increasing the pile of money in savings more than a new gadget."

"Saving is a highly addictive activity and you should consider it carefully before you begin. Once you start doing it, it will be like a gateway drug. Soon, without warning, you will start reading books about investing. You will find yourself looking at real estate listings for investment opportunities. You will start looking for business opportunities. You might even seriously consider starting a business yourself.

"Before you know it, you will be on your way to accumulating real wealth, so be very sure that you want to go down this path before you start saving money. If you do not want to suffer the consequences of financial freedom and abundance, then do not start keeping some of your paycheck. Just stay safe and continue to spend it all."

LESSON: Eat your dinner first and soon you will have more dessert than you can eat!

CHAPTER FOURTEEN
The Basic Formula

It was a Friday afternoon and Tommy was sitting on his front porch doing his homework when he noticed the Old Man talking to another man leaning on an old pickup truck in front of the Old Man's house. He had witnessed the same scene pretty much every Friday since he moved in next door.

Every Friday, the same man would arrive at the Old Man's house at about the same time of day, unload a lawn mower, and cut the lawn. Then he would take out his trimmer and trim the grass around the trees and sidewalk. He would trim along the fences. Then he would trim the trees and the bushes, rake up the debris and blow the cut grass from the sidewalk with his backpack blower.

Tommy had watched the man do this same thing many times, and he was impressed with the man's workmanship. The Old Man's yard always looked impeccable when he was finished.

The part he found interesting, though, was not how nice the yard looked. The Old Man often had skilled people working at his house. He was not lazy or incapable of taking care of his home himself, but he believed in having things done by those best qualified to do them for the best possible results.

What interested Tommy was how much the Old Man interacted particularly with this man. He would greet him warmly when he arrived with a hearty handshake and a smile, bring him a bottle of water while he worked, and would spend a considerable amount of time talking with him before he left. Tommy wasn't close enough to hear their conversations, but they didn't seem like small talk, these two men were clearly long-time friends with a lot to talk about.

Tommy decided to ask the Old Man about the landscaper during their usual lesson the next day.

Tommy still wasn't a fan of getting up early on a Saturday for his sessions with the Old Man, but he knew better than to make the him wait. He called it "a dollar waiting on a dime" or something like that. Tommy had made that mistake once and he didn't care to repeat it!

He sat in his usual spot on the couch and waited quietly while the Old Man fixed his cup of coffee and came into the living room. Once the Old Man sat down and set his cup on his desk, Tommy knew it was time to begin, but before the Old Man could start speaking, Tommy asked about the scene he had witnessed the previous afternoon.

"That lawn guy really does a good job on your lawn. How much do you pay him for that?" Tommy asked.

Uncertain of the reason for Tommy's sudden interest in his lawn, the Old Man decided that it was probably not a good idea to discourage Tommy's curiosity, so he answered plainly. "Fifty dollars. I have been trying to pay him more for years, but he won't let me."

Tommy had only been learning about money and life from the Old Man for a short while now, but he knew enough to recognize two problems with that answer.

"Let me get this straight. He only charges you fifty dollars for all that work? And you want to pay him more, but he won't take more?" Tommy was struggling to figure out which of these old men was the dumb one and concluded that they were both a bit "off." He was smart enough to keep this observation to himself, however.

Sarcastically, Tommy quipped, "Maybe that guy should come over here on Saturday instead of on Friday, so he could learn some business stuff like me."

The Old Man laughed so loudly that Tommy flinched. It was easily the loudest sound he had ever heard the Old Man make, and that was saying something. Tommy was certain his joke wasn't that funny, so he was also certain that a long-winded sermon was about to come his way.

"I can promise you one thing young man, if Walter Schmidt came here on a Saturday for a lesson about how money works, I would be sitting right there on that couch beside you, and Walter would be sitting in this chair right here, teaching us both. That man taught me the basic formula that that is the foundation of everything I know about money and business.

"If it wasn't for him, I wouldn't have anything to teach you," began the story that would be this day's lesson and arguably the most important lesson Tommy ever learned from the Old Man. He told Tommy that when he had graduated from high school, he needed a job. Walter had graduated a few years before him and had started his landscape business as soon as he finished school. His business was doing quite well, but he didn't need any more help at that time.

Walter did, however, like young Hollis and wanted to help him. He knew another guy who had a swimming pool installation business. The work was seasonal for the most part, and it was physically demanding, but the man was always needing more help and would likely hire him with a good reference from Walter.

Hollis thanked Walter for his help and was about to leave to go talk to the other man to ask about a job. Walter stopped him and asked what his plan was. When the youngster didn't reply, Walter offered to introduce him personally to his friend with the swimming pool business, and to buy him lunch on the way there.

Hollis was broke, and hungry, so he gratefully accepted the generous offer.

They drove to a local drive-in restaurant that sold what were generally regarded as the best hotdogs in the state. Walter encouraged him to order as much as he could eat, and hungry young Hollis obliged him.

"You are a good guy, and I like your spirit. I think you have a lot of potential, but if you don't have a plan for your life, you will become a part of someone else's plan and you won't like how that ends up for you," Walter said. "I can't give you a specific plan for your life. That is up to you and only you, but I would like to share with you a basic formula that my father shared with me when I graduated from high school. It should help you make your plan."

Hollis's mouth was full, so he simply nodded and smiled. He was eating a huge plate of free food from a friend who was bringing him to likely get hired for his first real job, so refusing to listen wasn't really an option.

Walter explained. "Right now, you have no skills and no tools and no money. What you do have is time. So, what you do now is sell your time and labor to someone else who needs it.

You save your money and don't buy anything that you don't absolutely need. Anything. While you are working, you watch the other people working around you, especially the ones making more money than you make, the people with skills and talents. When you learn some new skills, you make more money. You save more money and you still don't buy anything you don't need. That part is real important, got it? Once you have some skills, you buy some tools to help you get more work done in less time. Now you get paid for your time, your skills, and your tools and you make even more money. Now, you can buy a few things, but still save as much as you can.

"You keep saving until you have enough to start your own business. Then you make more money once again. You keep saving that money until you have enough money to start buying things that make you money while you are doing something else. When you have enough things making money for you, then you can stop working with your body and keep making money with your money and your brain instead! Then you are back to where you started. You have nothing but time, but it will be different, much different."

Young Hollis admitted that he didn't totally grasp what Walter had told him, but he understood the general idea and knew what he had to do first.

He got the job working on the pool crew. The owner paid him eight dollars an hour. His job mainly consisted of digging and wheelbarrowing, which was tough physically, especially in the summer heat of "pool season," but Hollis was focused on the next step, so he never complained.

As he worked, he watched the other guys on the crew closely, especially the more experienced guys assembling the pool, leveling it, installing the liners, and putting the filter systems together. He listened as the owner explained to customers how everything worked and answered their questions. He paid attention to how much the owner charged for different jobs and what everything cost.

As he got better at his tasks, and completed them quicker, he started to help with the more advanced aspects of the installations. Whenever someone didn't come into work or quit, Hollis jumped right in and helped fill the gaps left by the absent workers, while making sure to never miss work himself. He made sure the jobs were completed correctly and on time.

Soon enough, the owner recognized his efforts and hired a new guy to do Hollis's job and promoted him, raising his pay to twelve dollars an hour. He continued to save his money and paid attention to every detail of the jobs he was working on, especially how the owner handled problems that arose. He learned the solutions to common problems, and a general attitude about figuring out those solutions for himself.

After a few months, the owner offered him the opportunity to run a second crew on his own if he could buy a truck and the necessary tools to equip a crew. Hollis had been saving his money as Walter had instructed him to do, so he was ready when the offer came.

For the rest of that first season, he was leading his own installation crew, often completing two installations in a single day. Even after paying his workers, paying for materials, and splitting the remainder with the owner, he was making several hundred dollars a day.

When the next season came around, Hollis had saved enough to start his own pool installation company. The money he earned from that company became the money he used to buy his first rental property.

"I owe Walter Schmidt a debt I can never repay, Tommy," the Old Man explained. What he taught me changed the course of my entire life, and come to think of it, yours too. That is why I laughed so hard when you suggested that I could teach him something about business and money."

Tommy was impressed with the story and he had taken lots of notes while the Old Man was talking, but there was still something bothering him. Something didn't quite add up to him.

"If he knows so much about business and you owe him such a huge debt, why does he cut your grass for fifty dollars and drive that old truck?" Tommy asked.

"Well, about the time I started buying rental properties and accumulating some money, Walter came to see me. His business was doing great, but if he wanted to grow more, he would have to start doing bigger jobs, not just small lawns like mine. To do that, he would need more equipment. He would need bigger mowers, and he would need to have help with the contracts and paperwork involved in bigger jobs. He had some money saved, of course, but he also had a new wife, a new house, and a new baby.

"Since I knew he was good at his business and a man of great integrity, I loaned him the money to get the equipment he needed, and I asked my lawyer to help him with the contracts and paperwork that were involved. Because he had taught me so much, I couldn't charge him interest for the loan and told him to pay me when the bigger jobs started paying off. He is a proud man, so he insisted on giving me a fifty percent discount on my landscape needs for life instead of interest. He wouldn't take no for an answer, so I agreed."

"Since he is still cutting your grass so cheap and driving that old truck, I guess it didn't really work out for him, huh? That is too bad, he seems super nice," Tommy said sadly.

The Old Man took a sip of his coffee and stood up. He said, "Come on, Tommy, let's go for a ride. It is too nice of a day to stay inside all day anyway. Let's go get some lunch, I know a place nearby with the best hotdogs."

Not one to turn down a hotdog, Tommy jumped to his feet and headed for the front door. When they got to the end of the street, the Old Man turned towards the high school instead of towards downtown where the restaurant was located.

"Before we eat, I have to make a few quick stops. There is something I want you to see that I bet you never noticed before," the Old Man said.

When they pulled into the high school parking lot, the place was empty except for a few workers cutting the grass. One was riding a huge mower, one was trimming around the edges of the fences and trees, another was trimming the trees and bushes, and the last one was blowing the cut grass from the sidewalks and the parking lot. The Old Man pointed to the large box truck parked across the parking lot.

"Tommy, my eyes are getting old, what does that truck say over there, across the lot?" asked the Old Man.

Tommy looked straight ahead, squinted his eyes and smiled broadly. "Schmidt Landscaping" "Huh." was all the Old Man said.

They left the school parking lot and headed towards downtown. They pulled into the parking lot of the recently completed children's hospital. Tommy was getting the idea, so he looked around and saw at least six men and women working on the landscaping around the hospital. He looked around more and soon spotted another box truck, this one even bigger than the one at the high school. "Schmidt Landscaping" once again. The Old Man didn't say a word, he simply drove out of the parking lot.

"One more stop, Tommy, and then we can get those hotdogs I promised."

He drove a few more blocks towards downtown and pulled into the parking lot of a strip mall. It held a dozen businesses, ranging from a small restaurant to a hair salon. The Old Man drove around the left side of the building to a larger lot in the rear. At the back of the lot sat a huge metal building that looked like an airplane hangar. In letters as big as Tommy, the sign read "Schmidt Landscaping." There were several large box trucks parked outside, some with their hoods open and feet dangling out of them.

Inside the huge open bay doors, were a bunch of mowers and other equipment in various stages of repair. The Old Man tapped Tommy on the shoulder and pointed to the back of the strip mall building. "There isn't a sign with his name on it, but Walter owns that building also."

The two began walking towards the building in the direction of the smaller door on the right that read "office." As soon as they entered, Walter rose out of his chair with a huge smile and embraced the Old Man. He smiled at Tommy and shook his hand. Tommy instantly liked him and noticed that he seemed younger up close. Tommy was a curious young man and he couldn't help but ask the obvious question.

"Pardon me for asking, Mr. Schmidt, but why do you cut this guy's grass yourself instead of just sending one of your crews to do it?"

Walter Schmidt looked at Tommy and chuckled. "Because I like to talk, and no one else will listen to me anymore except for this old man right here." he said, pointing to the Old Man with a smile.

---

*LESSON: You must have a plan or
get stuck in someone else's plan.*

CHAPTER FIFTEEN
Assets Are in The Eyes
of The Beholder

The Old Man was determined to teach Tommy the vocabulary he would need to successfully navigate the world of money and investing. He had already taught him about stocks and bonds. He had already experienced having a small business venture and having some semi-passive income.

He wanted to teach Tommy about assets but was struggling with exactly how to approach the subject in a way that would be easy for the kid to absorb but would still be meaningful to him.

He didn't want to just teach him the textbook definitions or even the more evolved definitions popular today.

A textbook might say that an asset is something that has value. Others say that an asset is something that makes money, and that is a more useful definition, but he still wanted to make a finer distinction than those meanings.

He didn't want to bore Tommy to death with terms like depreciating assets, appreciating assets, and so on. He wanted to give Tommy a broader and more prosperous-thinking definition, but he was stuck as to how to do it.

Then, one day, as he was trying to focus on the problem, his mind kept wandering off to a conversation he'd had recently with a close friend. The topic was a political one and the two friends had totally opposing views, which they had been "expressing" to each other for years.

On this occasion, his friend shared with him a personal experience that was clearly the basis of his opinion. It made the Old Man examine where his own opinion came from, and how he formed it. Once he uncovered the source of his own strongly held beliefs, he was able to see how his friend came to the opposite conclusion on the same topic.

Their experiences directly led to their positions. Now he realized that both positions made perfect sense to those holding them in the context of their personal experience. If the two could swap experiences, they would likely swap views as well.

This gave him the insight he needed to teach Tommy about assets.

He had given Tommy a few books to read, and although he didn't read them as diligently as the Old Man would like, he knew that Tommy had read the first few books and had at least a book definition of assets in his head.

"Tommy, do you know what assets are?" he asked.

Tommy thought for a moment and said, "Assets are things that are worth money".

The Old Man said, "Yes, that is true. That is exactly how most adults would define the word, but I want to teach you something else about that word that might be helpful to you"

Tommy liked it when the Old Man taught him something that not all adults knew. He realized that if he only learned what everyone else knew, he would end up where everyone else ended up.

"Tommy, I want you to remember this phrase. An asset is in the eye of the beholder," the Old Man said.

Tommy looked confused, so the Old Man continued, "Whether or not something is an asset depends on the person holding the asset. An asset could be anything. It could be money. It could be a tool. It could be an idea. It could be a relationship or a connection. It could be a situation. Whether or not you can make money with something depends on you and your ability to spot and create opportunities. That same thing might be worthless to someone else, but be worth millions to you because of how you think"

Tommy was interested now, but he would need more information before the concept would really sink in. He needed an example he could wrap his head around.

"Remember when you sold that gum in school?" asked the Old Man.

Tommy grinned as he recalled his first profitable business venture. "Sure do. That was fun." "In that case, you turned a relationship with your mom's boyfriend into an asset. Because you got him to sell you candy at a wholesale price, you were able to form a profitable venture. Do you think anyone else knew the same guy and what he did for a living?"

"Probably so," answered Tommy.

"But no one else thought of a way to connect that knowledge with a way to make money like you did, did they? Any other kid could have done the same thing you did, but they didn't." the Old Man didn't think it important that he take credit for the idea.

He gave some more examples to reinforce the concept. "In my old clumsy hands, a surgical scalpel would be worthless. Less than worthless, even. It would just be dangerous. But, in the hands of a skilled surgeon, that same scalpel is a priceless asset, capable of saving lives and making a lot of money for the surgeon."

"An electrician's tools would be useless to me but could provide an electrician with a great income. If a man buys a stock for $50 and it goes up to a $100, it was an asset for him, but if I buy it at $100, and it drops to $50, it wasn't really an asset for me, was it?"

He paused for a minute to make sure Tommy was getting the idea. The boy sat quietly, then nodded and smiled, indicating that he understood, and was encouraged by the idea of possessing the power to turn nearly anything into an asset with the power of his own mind.

Though Tommy seemed to have the idea, the Old Man wanted to help him grasp the full power of it, so he took him for a ride around town. As they walked to the car, he pointed at his lawn. "See that grass growing? To the landscaper that means money to be made, an asset. To me, it is an expense, but to him, it is an asset because it produces income."

Once they got into town and got stuck in traffic, he pointed to the taxi in front of them. "See that car, the taxi? To that taxi driver, it is an asset. See that nice car, with the family inside, next to it? That car is much nicer, but it is not an asset, it costs those folks money, likely a lot of it.

"Sometimes, things can be an asset to more than one person," the Old Man said as he stopped in front of a house on a side street near the middle of town.

"See that house there, Tommy? A few years ago, I bought that land and had that house built on it. I sold the house and made some money. That piece of land was an asset to me, but it was also an asset to the man who sold it to me. He had bought it years ago for much less than I paid him for it. It also became an asset to the people who bought the house from me, because the house and the land are worth more now than when I sold it to them. When you can turn one resource into an asset for several, or even many people, then you can really start to make a difference and make some big money. The people who can use their knowledge and skills to turn the resources that are all around us into assets that benefit the people around them become the truly prosperous, the super wealthy. Tommy, that is what I am trying to teach you: how to become one of those people. Now, how about a hotdog and an ice cream?"

LESSON: Nearly any resource can become an asset.
An asset is in the eye of the beholder.

CHAPTER SIXTEEN
Economic Freedom

Tommy had really enjoyed his last lesson about assets. He felt empowered by the idea that he could use his brain and his creativity to turn resources all around him into assets that produce income. Knowing that there were potential assets literally everywhere was inspiring to him. He was a little concerned that very few people seemed to share these ideas and thoughts.

Why don't more people look around and come up with good ideas? He questioned. As he pondered this question, he remembered another one that had been in the back of his head since he left the Old Man's house after his last lesson.

"How many of these assets does a person need to be rich?" he asked, in his usual straightforward way.

"Well, Tommy, the answer is close to the answer of 'what is an asset?'. The truth is that what makes a person rich, wealthy, or prosperous is largely up to each person to decide for himself," the Old Man answered.

"For some people, being rich means they have enough passive income coming to them to cover their expenses whether they go to work or not. To some people, it is a certain dollar amount they have saved. One person might feel rich with a few thousand dollars in the bank, and another might feel poor with a million dollars in the bank."

The Old Man explained, "I have a different definition of financial freedom than most people. Having a certain amount of passive income is an excellent start, but incomes and assets are still vulnerable to circumstances. The company that pays a dividend might eliminate the dividend if business gets bad. A renter might not pay the rent. A prosperous business might experience hardships and stop being profitable. All manner of even the most stable passive income is still vulnerable to unforeseen events.

"True prosperity is both a feeling and a level of confidence. True prosperity, as a feeling, occurs when a person feels like they have what they need and want and are comfortable helping others. They have enough that they feel like they can share without hurting their own lifestyle. A person can achieve this feeling at dollar amounts far below the million-dollar mark. There is an old saying, 'If you have more than you need, build a longer table, not a higher fence'.

"Some people have deep-seated insecurities about money that keep them from ever experiencing this feeling, no matter how much they accumulate. Many other folks might deride them as being greedy because they don't seem to share their wealth with others, but the whole truth can be much more complicated than that.

"The reason many people do not ever reach the level of feeling prosperous is that they have not fully reached the level of confidence in their abilities to produce income from their mental efforts as they have that they can produce from their physical efforts. They are worried that they can no longer do the work that brought the money to them in the first place.

"That makes the money they have irreplaceable in their minds. In most cases, this is a valid concern. If their wealth was accumulated mostly through old-fashioned brute force work, they are probably correct in deciding that they cannot replace that money if it were lost, spent, or shared with others.

"What may look like greed to others, is really just completely justified and valid fear. If a person works their entire lifetime accumulating enough money to last them through the rest of their lives, it is totally understandable why they would be reluctant to put themselves in a vulnerable position by giving away what they cannot readily replace.

"What the Old Man, my mentor, tried to instill in me was the idea of 'true prosperity,' which was not only the feeling of having enough to comfortably share with others, but also the confidence that I could replace those funds I gave away at any time through the application of my talents and skills and knowledge. Those are resources that age quite well, and even improve with age. More experience tends to add more wisdom to these resources and makes them more powerful and more effective.

"Tommy, what he and I both knew, and I am trying to teach you, is that we could lose all our money today and be back where we were financially within a few short years because the skills we used to accumulate the wealth in the first place were still with us and had even grown stronger through repeated use.

"We knew that most of their accumulated wealth resulted from deals we put together like the ones we worked on in the real estate business. Our physical contributions to these deals were mainly confined to signing documents and making decisions. These are things people can do even in their older years!

"If a person really seeks to be economically free and financially independent, there may not be a dollar amount that would suffice. Any amount of money can be lost, a fact to which any former lottery winner who is currently broke can attest. If a person truly wants to be free, they must acquire skills and talents that do not decline with age and are sufficient to produce income reliably. It is preferable to develop more than one such talent, but a single strong one is a good start. One must constantly remain vigilant for changes in the economy, both locally, nationally, and globally. A prosperous person knows that every event, negative or positive, carries within it an opportunity.

"Every change, no matter how subtle, creates a new need that a person can fill, and create an income while doing so. A new tax law change makes those who understand it best quite valuable to those who do not. People who recognize a way that the tax law creates a new, more profitable way to structure an existing business or form a new one can make a lot of money for themselves and others.

"The bottom line, Tommy, is that wealth and prosperity are not dollar amounts or income amounts, they are levels of thinking, confidence and skills that we each determine for ourselves. No one else can dictate to us when we should feel prosperous or wealthy. Truthfully, the feeling itself tends to attract the reality.

LESSON: We decide for ourselves when we are prosperous enough to share. We can declare ourselves prosperous whenever we wish.

CHAPTER SEVENTEEN
John L. Williams

Tommy was more excited than usual for this week's session with the Old Man for two reasons: The Old Man had asked him to come on a Sunday instead of Saturday and told him to bring a jacket. This meant he would finally find out where the Old Man went on Sunday mornings. He knew the Old Man wasn't religious, so it wasn't church. It also meant that they would be going somewhere outdoors instead of the Old Man's stuffy living room for a change.

When Tommy arrived on Sunday morning, the Old Man was ready to go. He had his jacket on and was dangling the keys to his car from his finger aimed in Tommy's direction. Tommy always enjoyed driving the Old Man's car because he knew that he was the only human besides the Old Man himself who did so. He'd been doing it since he got his license two years ago.

They got in the car and the Old Man told Tommy to head towards the park near the high school. The park was a simple one. It had several picnic benches and a few tables where the older folks played chess and talked on the end near the parking lot, and basketball courts, tennis courts, and a pond at the far end near the high school.

Tommy and the Old man were about to sit down at the nearest bench and begin their lesson when an older pickup truck pulled into the parking lot and parked next to the Old Man's car. The Old Man told Tommy to wait while he got up and walked towards the newly arrived pickup truck. He greeted the driver and walked him back to the bench where Tommy sat. The man was quite a bit older than the Old Man, but he had the same bright eyes that indicated his mind was sharp. Tommy thought it was nice of the Old Man to meet the older man at his car instead of just waiting for him at the table.

When the two men sat down, they were already chatting away like people who hadn't seen each other in a long time. The older man nodded and smiled at Tommy and the two men made it clear that they intended to keep talking, so Tommy looked around the park to see what else was going on. It was clear that his lesson was going to have to wait, but he didn't mind too much, as it was a beautiful day outside.

He noticed some kids from school playing basketball, so he politely excused himself and went to join them. He looked back at the two old men occasionally, waiting for a sign that their conversation was over, and his lesson could begin. After several hours, the two men stood up and shook hands, and the Old Man walked the other man to his car and waved as he drove away.

The Old Man motioned for Tommy to join him at the car in the lot, and Tommy realized that his lesson for the day was just not coming, which didn't bother him too much because at least he learned where the Old Man went on Sundays. One mystery about the Old Man down, several dozen left to go, he figured.

"I guess we can save today's lesson for next Saturday, then?" Tommy asked.

"What do you mean today's lesson, Tommy?" the Old Man replied. "Today's lesson is over, we have other stuff to discuss next week."

Tommy was confused and said so. "You just got so caught up talking to that other man, I just figured you forgot about the lesson."

"That was the lesson, Tommy," came the reply.

The Old Man asked him what he had noticed about the other man and their conversation. Tommy shared that the other man was neatly dressed, but not in a particularly fancy way. His truck was older, but neat and seemed to run smoothly. He observed that while the men talked a lot, it seemed that the conversation was mostly one-sided, with the other man doing most of the talking and the Old Man hardly getting a word in edgewise.

Tommy said that he noticed how the Old Man was very polite, even deferential, towards the older man. He quickly added that the

Old Man wasn't rude to other people, but that he was just more noticeably polite to the older man. It wasn't something Tommy had seen before from the Old Man.

"Those are all good observations, Tommy, but what did you learn?" The Old Man asked. "That there is at least one person on this Earth that can talk more than you?" Tommy joked.

"I know you are kidding, but you are closer than you know to the truth," answered the Old Man. "Tommy, even though I am your teacher, I am still also a student. To continue growing our wealth and our prosperity, we must continue our personal growth by adding to our wisdom. To stop learning is to stop growing, and to stop growing is to start dying."

Tommy knew that the Old Man was an avid reader, but he never considered the fact that he might still be learning from other people. The Old Man further explained that when you are talking, you are not learning. You learn the most when someone else is talking and that is why the Old Man was mostly listening at the park.

"So that is where you go on Sundays, huh?" Tommy asked.

"Yes, but I fear that I may not have my mentor for much longer. His physical health is failing, though his mind is still sharp. There is still a lot I would like to know from him." The Old Man said quietly.

Tommy was still having trouble picturing the Old Man as a student. He had even more difficulty picturing the humbly dressed older man he met as a teacher to the Old Man. He just had to ask.

"Who is that man, anyway?" asked Tommy

"You know that new children's hospital they built downtown a few years ago, the big one?" asked the Old Man. Tommy nodded. "Do you remember the full name of it, Tommy?"

"I sure do, it is called the John L. Williams Regional Children's Hospital" Tommy said proudly.

"That man was John L. Williams, or as I call him, the Old Man."

LESSON: Learning should be a lifelong habit. If we stop learning, we stop growing. If we stop growing, we start dying.

CHAPTER EIGHTEEN
Salty Soup

Tommy's mother had called the night before and warned the Old Man that Tommy would not be in a very good mood for his Saturday visit. She explained that Tommy and his girlfriend, Theresa, had a huge fight. They had been dating for two years- which is like ten years for teenagers- and it was uncertain if their relationship was going to survive this fight. They had argued before, but this one wasn't just an argument or disagreement, it was a fight.

The Old Man decided he would set aside the lesson he had planned for Tommy and instead started making a pot of his famous chicken noodle soup, Tommy's favorite. The Old Man hoped he could cheer up his young friend with food.

Tommy must have smelled the soup cooking, because he came in the kitchen door instead of his usual entrance, the front door. The Old Man could see how distressed Tommy was, and silently gestured to the table, where he had bowls, spoons, and crackers already laid out.

The Old Man said, "The soup needs to simmer a minute more, want to talk about it?"

Tommy figured his mother had told the Old Man about the fight already, so there was no point in avoiding the subject. The Old Man was consistent. He wouldn't want to talk about another subject until the obvious one was talked about first. Simmering was a good strategy for soup, but not always for problems.

"Theresa and I had a huge fight. Honestly, I am not even sure what it was about or how it even started." Tommy told him.

"I bet you remember how it ended, though, don't you?" The Old Man replied.

"The last thing she said was 'I never want to see your face again!'" came the answer. "What was the last thing you said?" the Old Man knew this was the significant part. "She was being dumb, so I told her so!" explained Tommy.

The Old Man knew these two kids had been dating for a while. He knew they loved each other and he thought they were a good match. He was genuinely heartbroken for them, Tommy and Theresa. Sincere love doesn't come around often, so it is precious, and should be nurtured whenever possible, not just by those in love, but by those who care for them. The Old Man had been married for several decades before his wife passed away, and he still missed her every day in the years since she died.

He understood Tommy's pain and easily recognized the young man's mistake. He decided to show him instead of just telling him. The Old Man believed that the most important lessons couldn't just be spoken. They sometimes had to involve other senses to be effective.

"Grab your bowl and come get some of this soup." The Old Man waved Tommy over to the stove. Tommy wasn't very hungry, but he knew better than to pass up the soup the Old Man made just for him under any circumstances. He ladled out a little more than half a bowl and sat down. The Old Man waited for Tommy to take his first spoonful. "How is it?" he asked.

"Perfect as always," came the reply.

The Old Man reached over and picked up the salt shaker from the other end of the table. He sprinkled a single shake into Tommy's bowl. Tommy was confused but said nothing.

"Try it again." The Old Man told him.

Tommy was a little nervous. Was the Old Man finally losing his mind? He took another taste and said, "Little salty, but still good."

The Old Man reached for the shaker again. This time, he shook the shaker several times, vigorously, into Tommy's bowl. Tommy sat back and looked at the Old man as if he had just grown a second head. Certainly, he has lost it, thought Tommy.

"Try it again." The Old Man commanded. "But it's,"

The Old Man cut him off. "Try it again!" he insisted.

Tommy did as he was told and took just a little taste. Predictably, the soup was inedible. "You ruined it." Tommy accused.

"No, Tommy, you did." The Old Man answered firmly.

The Old Man explained, "Tommy that bowl of soup represents your relationship with Theresa. When I sprinkled a little salt into it, that represented a normal argument or disagreement. Calling Theresa 'dumb' was your way of dumping way too much salt into the soup. A strong relationship can survive many arguments, but few insults."

"There is a huge difference between disagreeing with someone and insulting someone personally. People can withstand having their thoughts and ideas challenged if they have a normal measure of self-esteem and if they feel like the other people still like them. They may even change their mind on a subject if they find the other ideas compelling enough. But, if they are insulted, they feel like you are attacking who they are, and not just one of their ideas, and that is much more difficult for anyone to handle.

"People can be around other people who do not like all their ideas, but no one wants to be around other people who do not like them personally. Calling someone dumb tells them that you don't like them very much."

Tommy knew the Old Man was right and he desperately wanted to fix things with Theresa.

He knew from previous lessons with the Old Man that the good news about being responsible for something is that if you are responsible for breaking it, you get the opportunity to fix it also. "How do you fix a bowl of salty soup? Isn't it ruined forever?" Tommy asked.

The Old Man told Tommy to get the other big soup pot from the cabinet. He had Tommy get the carrots and the celery from the refrigerator. He sat at the kitchen table and continued to instruct Tommy. He told Tommy how to cut the chicken and the vegetables. He had him fill the pot with water and boil the noodles. Tommy had never made soup before, but he was interested to see where this lesson was going.

Step by step, the Old Man talked Tommy through the recipe for his famous chicken noodle soup. He hadn't shared it with anyone before now. When Tommy complained that the Old Man wasn't helping, the Old Man told him, "This is your mess to fix, not mine." After an hour or so of preparations, the soup was boiling. Soon after, the Old Man told Tommy to turn the heat down and let it simmer for a little while.

The Old Man walked to the table and picked up the salty bowl of soup and poured it directly into the pot of new soup. He stirred it thoroughly. Then, he offered Tommy a taste with his wooden spoon. Tommy was surprised to notice that the soup was nearly perfect. He understood what this meant. He had to apologize and then "dilute" his bad behavior with an overwhelming amount of good behavior and actions.

The Old Man gave him the address of the florist that had helped him so many times when he needed "a new pot of soup" and explained the power of a gesture to Tommy.

LESSON: Words are powerful, choose yours carefully in case you end up eating them!

Chapter Nineteen
What Is FICA Anyway?

Tommy had received his first paycheck on a Friday afternoon around 3 pm. At 3:30 pm, he was knocking at the Old Man's front door. Of course, the Old Man and Tommy had discussed taxes during their lessons, but sometimes the reality of an academic lesson coming to life can be jarring to young folks entering the work force. Tommy had in hand the slip that had been attached to his paycheck that showed all his tax deductions and was clearly upset and confused.

"Exactly what is FICA, and why did it take so much of my money?"

The Old Man motioned for Tommy to follow him into the kitchen, so he could prepare a cup of coffee as he gave his student an unscheduled impromptu lesson on the American tax system.

He had seriously considered warning Tommy about payroll taxes to save him this experience, but he found that a student's willingness to learn a topic increased substantially when the topic was timely and relevant, like the moment you see your first paycheck! Tommy was all ears right now, and this lesson would stick better than when it was a strictly academic exercise.

The Old Man went through the various deductions on his paycheck slip and explained what each one was for, but he decided that it was much more important for the young man to fully grasp the way our tax system works so, as they often did, they took a ride around town to make some observations and get a hotdog for old times' sake.

Tommy no longer needed someone to watch him on Saturdays, and the Old Man and Tommy had been spending much less time together for some years, but they were still close, and the Old Man had no intention of allowing Tommy to drift too far away from him and into the life of quiet mediocrity that awaited so many young folks.

Still, it was also important for Tommy to experience the same things that other folks experienced as far as basic financial realities and struggles. If Tommy never felt the shock of seeing his hard-earned money disappear through taxation and other expenses, he would never be an effective instructor, no matter how much knowledge he possessed or how much he cared about his students. When he told people that he felt their pain, they had to believe him.

"Those taxes that you paid feel painful, and I know that you probably even feel a little bit cheated as many folks do when they get their first check. Heck, some people feel that way with every check!" the Old Man began. "But that money we all pay in taxes is very important to all of us and our way of living. Without taxes, none of us would have a paycheck at all."

As they drove, the Old Man pointed at the road they were riding on, "Taxes paved this road." He drove past the high school from which Tommy had recently graduated. "Taxes built that school and paid the teachers who teach there." They drove past the fire station and the police station in town. "Taxes built those buildings and pays those police and firefighters too."

"Tommy, if you didn't have these roads to drive on, that school to learn in, those cops and firefighters to keep you safe, the bridges to carry you over rivers and streams, do you really think you would have a job to go to?" asked the Old Man.

Tommy was starting to get the idea, "No, I guess not" he answered sheepishly.

"Those tax dollars we all contribute are why we have such a nice country to live in. They are what creates a safe atmosphere where we can all build businesses and prosper. They provide healthcare in our old age through programs like Medicare, when the health insurance companies won't provide coverage for us anymore or would charge more than we could afford to pay.

"They provide some money in our later years even if we don't save any ourselves, so we don't starve. That money pays the folks in the military that keep us safe. Heck, some of it even pays those brilliant politicians who make so many amazing decisions and laws!" He smiled widely as he included that last group.

By now Tommy felt a little bit guilty about complaining, as he realized he had benefitted from other people's tax money his whole life and was whining about the very first few dollars he contributed on his own. The Old Man sensed this and decided to shift gears a little bit. He had made one point, and it was time to make another.

"That being said Tommy, while it is vitally important and even patriotic for every American to pay what taxes he owes, it is not smart or patriotic to pay more than you are obligated to pay." He once again had Tommy's full attention.

The Old Man went on to explain to Tommy how the entire tax system was basically constructed as an incentive program geared towards building wealth and prosperity. It was literally designed to forcefully guide American citizens to wealth if followed as it was intended.

"Tommy, the system of taxes basically tells us that if we choose to remain employees and settle for a life of mediocrity and constant struggle, we are free to do so, but if we do choose that life, we will suffer the consequences by paying a larger share of our income back to the government in the form of taxes. There is nothing wrong morally with wanting to work for someone else all your life. Many fine people do exactly that, but there is a penalty to be paid for that choice.

"If, however, a person chooses to seek a life of greater abundance and prosperity, the tax system is designed to help them do that. The system is structured so that the smarter you become and the wealthier you get, the less taxes you will pay, proportionately speaking. The more risk you take in terms of investing and business building, the more the government will reward that risk taking.

"As bad as the government is at many things, the one thing they are good at is rewarding those who seek to achieve wealth. Lawmakers understand that it is largely the risk takers who can succeed and build huge companies that employ lots of people who pay lots of taxes. Big businesses that sell lots of goods generate lots of sales taxes on those sales and income taxes from all the employees and other businesses supported by the one big business.

"Many folks gripe when they see a big business get bailed out or helped by the government, or when a large company declares bankruptcy and uses the laws to escape the results of bad business decisions. There are cases where this negative emotion is completely understandable. Abuse of the system is, without a doubt, a problem.

"However, without those safety nets in place, many folks who have the means and ability to take bigger risks to build bigger companies might choose not to take the risks if they stood to be destroyed by a single failure. Some of the greatest American companies ever built were built by individuals or groups with huge failures in their past. If their first failures had been allowed to crush them, the subsequent successes would never have happened. Where would we be if without all those companies that were the result of some entrepreneur's second, third, fourth try at building a company? Our country would be but a tiny fraction on the international success story it is now."

The Old Man was comfortable that Tommy understood both the significance of paying taxes and the desire to achieve a level of success that would be rewarded with a more favorable tax treatment.

Tommy seemed satisfied to pay his payroll taxes without griping, so that he could eventually learn more about ways to structure his finances in such a way that he took full advantage of the system that is designed to move him towards true prosperity.

The Old Man would revisit taxes again when Tommy was a bit older, but for now, knowing that there was a method to the apparent madness of taxes would have to suffice.

LESSON: The tax system is just an incentive system to guide us where we need to go to achieve prosperity.

CHAPTER TWENTY
Work Ethic

It had been a few weeks since the Old Man had helped Tommy understand how taxes worked and how important they were. Tommy had asked for a few minutes of his time to talk about a new issue that came up at work. Since this was Tommy's first job, the dynamics of the workplace were new to him. Having an actual boss and learning to do as he was told were causing the young man a little distress.

Tommy came into the living room and took his spot on the couch. He then launched into a twenty-minute non-stop tirade about how much he hated his job, hated his boss, hated the things he had to do, how unfair the whole job situation was. The Old Man, ever the optimist, smiled at Tommy and told him, "Good for you, Tommy. You are years ahead of schedule".

Tommy gave him the look he reserved for times like this when he was sure the Old Man had lost his mind completely.

"Yeah, some folks don't get that fed up with being an employee for at least 3-4 years. You managed to reach the same level in only a few weeks. You truly are an over-achiever, and I am so proud of you" he said with more than a hint of sarcasm.

"If I heard you right, one of your biggest issues is your boss, the assistant manager. He is always telling you to do things you don't want to do, is that right?" the Old Man asked.

Tommy was still upset, and he was certain the Old Man was going to make him feel worse before he made him feel better. It was kind of his pattern. "Yeah, since I am the newest guy, I get all the crappiest jobs to do."

"Did you already have them done before he asked?" replied the Old Man. "No, of course not. Why would I do that?" Tommy answered.

"So, if he didn't tell you, you wouldn't have done them? Did they need to be done?" continued the Old Man.

"Yes, they needed to be done and no, I wouldn't have done them without him telling me" Tommy was getting the familiar feeling that he knew where the Old Man was going with this line of questioning.

"Well, if you knew they needed doing, why didn't you just do them before being told?

Especially if you knew he was going to tell you soon anyway? Why wait to be told?" The Old Man had a valid point and Tommy knew it.

"That guy is doing you a huge favor, Tommy, and you should be grateful to him for it. He is teaching you discipline, and when you can transform the discipline he is teaching you, and imposing on you, into self-discipline, then you will be getting somewhere.

"Tommy, when we talk about starting your own business, what are some of the things about having your own business you look forward to the most?" He hoped Tommy wouldn't step right into this one, but he was disappointed.

"I can do what I want to do and not what someone else tells me, for one thing!"

"Once again, Tommy, you are way ahead of everyone else. Most people have no idea how or why their first business is going to fail, but you already have it figured out. Heck, now you can go ahead and start thinking about your second business attempt."

The Old Man explained, "Tommy, many new businesses fail in their first year or two. There are two main reasons businesses fail. The single biggest reason new businesses fail is because so many new business owners do exactly as you said you would do. They do the things they want to do instead of the things they have to do to keep their businesses alive.

"Most of the time, the things we least want to do are the very things that we must do to thrive.

All new business owners are in sales and calling on new customers can be tough. They would rather push some papers around and make some sales goals and call some friends for advice or go to long lunches every day.

"If you are a new business owner, you should be spending ninety-five percent of your time doing the things you are avoiding, like making sales calls. Your boss is teaching you to do the unpleasant tasks whether you want to do them or not. That is what I meant when I told you that your boss is doing you a favor.

"Having a business of your own does not mean you can do what you want, it means that you have no one else telling you what you need to do. That is now up to you. Going from being told what to do, and when, to having the self-discipline to do those things without being forced, is a tough change to make.

"Many folks fail because they fail to make the transition from imposed discipline to self- discipline. Starting a business does not make you freer, it makes you less free, at least at the beginning. This realization often comes too late for many who struggle with business ownership, especially if they were employees for a long time.

"Having a strong work ethic is important as an employee, but it is critical as an owner. Many people who have strong work ethics as employees suddenly find out the hard way that they owed a lot of the credit for that work ethic to the bosses that gave them little choice in the matter.

"They worked hard because their jobs depended on it, it was how they remained employed, and not necessarily an indicator of their own internal control mechanisms or strength of character.

"Before starting a business, a person must really dig deep inside to discover the self-discipline necessary to succeed. If your first response to the idea of having your own business is that you will get to what you want to do, you will likely fail quickly.

"The first key to being successful on your own is having the discipline to do all the things you do not want to do, as these are usually the tasks that bring in business and bring in the money you will need to stay in business. If you need to sell widgets, sell widgets all day long. Do the paperwork at night. Set your goals in the evenings. Spend your workday selling, selling, and finally, selling.

"Many studies indicate that the number one reason new businesses fail is that they are under- capitalized. In other words, they do not have enough money to survive long enough to get established and bring in needed revenues.

"Every time I read an article or hear someone repeat this as if it were true, I get irritated. My mentor taught me from his own observations and experience, the exact opposite is true. Most business fail because they have too much capital.

"As counter-intuitive as that may seem, the reason it is true is closely related to the first reason businesses fail. So many entrepreneurs spend months and years making business plans. They raise capital, they hire employees, they rent office space and sometimes warehouse space. They spend money on advertising, they hire professional help for accounting and office jobs.

"They spend a lot of time and money and then find out that no one wants their product or service and they fail. They don't fail because they didn't have enough money or resources, they failed because they had those resources.

"If they had no resources to start with, and they only had an idea for a product or service, they would be forced to generate the needed resources through the sale of that product or service. If they had a mortgage payment due and hungry kids, they would be out selling their product from dawn to dusk.

"If their product was worthy, people would buy it, and the money would come in, and they would be able to pay their bills and expand their business as much as their actual sales would support and dictate. My mentor was always talking about organic growth. Organic growth is what results when a product or service sells well and pays for its own business growth. It creates its own capital in the amounts needed to fuel the growth.

"Often, having a strong cushion of capital is the downfall of new businesses. Having a safety net gives people the luxury of stalling and not doing what they need to do, which is sell their products or services to paying clients. Everything else is secondary to that. If no one buys your products, then all the capital expenditure was a waste of money. If people do buy your products, then the revenue generated from those sales can be the capital.

"If you are a student and you have a paper due in two weeks, when do you finish that paper?

Yep, the night before it is due. That is human nature. If you have enough capital to last your new company six months without any sales, guess when you will get serious about sales? Yep, halfway through your fifth month, or about five and a half months too late to save you. People often mistake having access to capital for having a good business idea.

"If your idea is good, the capital will be a result of actual sales. If your idea is bad, no amount of capital will save you. The bonus to moving forward this way is that you will not lose all your money if you do not spend it all in advance and your idea sucks."

LESSON: Do not mistake imposed discipline for self-discipline. Owning a business means doing the unpleasant things first.

CHAPTER TWENTY-ONE
Managing Ego

Tommy and the Old Man were having breakfast at their favorite place, a fairly cheap restaurant that specialized in breakfast and was known for its casual atmosphere. It was a great place to talk and enjoy a homestyle meal. Tommy was filling the Old Man in on all the events of the previous week at work. ALL the events.

The Old Man noticed a pattern to Tommy's stories and the emotions that went with them. Tommy seemed to go quickly from being very proud of himself to being down in the dumps. His ego appeared to be somewhat fragile and subject to swinging back and forth between overconfidence and being overly humble, even distraught at times.

The Old Man had been trying to find a way to discuss this topic in a sensitive way, as he knew for a fact that the ego was the downfall of many an aspiring person. Folks can get cocky when things are going their way and despondent when things are not going their way. Both extremes usually lead to failure.

While they were talking, the Old Man heard two servers behind the counter talking. He wasn't eavesdropping, but the conversation was a bit animated, and the Old Man had a chronic case of "peripheral hearing." He often heard bits of other people's conversations when certain words or phrases caught his sub-conscious mind's attention.

One of the servers was a few years older than the other and seemed to be counseling the younger woman. The Old Man only heard a snippet of what she said, but it caught his attention. He heard her say "when you are in the valley, stand tall."

As he digested the tidbit, he surmised that there was a first part of that quote that would be helpful to his dilemma with Tommy. They finished their meal, and as they approached the register to pay their bill, the Old Man beckoned Tommy to come near and listen. He politely asked the woman if she could repeat for him the quote he had overheard.

She didn't seem at all surprised and told him, "When you are on the mountaintop, bow down low. When you are in the valley, stand tall!" The Old Man thanked her profusely and explained that he had been struggling with a way to express exactly that sentiment for months now. Her quote said it perfectly. He handed her some money and thanked her for her wisdom and for sharing it with him.

Tommy had watched the entire exchange with some curiosity and sensed that his lesson for the day had only begun. He was right.

The Old Man explained "Tommy, the human ego is both powerful and dangerous. Without a conscious effort to manage it, it can destroy careers, lives, and businesses faster than any outside circumstances. Many an empire has been toppled and laid to ruin by the ravages of an ego running wild.

"Having some success has the unfortunate side effect of convincing the human ego that it is the reason for the success that hard work and planning earned. The ego says to a person, 'you are special.' The ego inflates itself and crowds out the real reasons for one's successes and replaces them with some notion of supremacy and destiny. It tells us that we will continue to succeed not because of what we do, but simply because of who we are, and it falsely uses recent successes as evidence.

"Believing you are special and that you are somehow imbued with unique qualities unknown to others is a dangerous thing to believe. Not only is it demonstrably untrue, the notion is offensive to everyone around you. Ego forgets how we got where we are, how many people helped us along the way, how many customers, employees, family members participated.

"Ego tells us that we did it by ourselves and we don't need any help. When we are on the mountaintop, our ego tells us to puff out our chests and hold our heads high and rejoice in ourselves.

"The result of this nonsense is as predictable as it is sad to witness. Those who helped us get to the top suddenly lose interest in helping us further. The same ego that tells us we are special blocks us from receiving new information, from learning what we need to maintain our spot on the mountain and what we need to learn to climb the next mountain.

"Ego cuts us off from the very resources we used to achieve our goal. Like an army whose supply lines have been disrupted, our downfall is inevitable. Being in a successful place, one that we have worked hard to achieve, is a signal to us, if we are smart, to double down on the humility that got us there in the first place.

"When you are at your highest level is when you should look around for people to thank and praise for their help. Dance with those who brought you to the dance.

"Quite often, sports teams who win championships soon suffer from this very malady.

Players who were humble enough to give their all to the team effort start to overestimate their individual contribution to the win. They begin to see themselves as a bigger part of the victory than is accurate.

"Even worse, sometimes their evaluation is indeed accurate, but speaking it out loud poisons the very atmosphere of teamwork and cooperation that won them the championship in the first place. As each player jockeys for their portion of the credit, the spirit that won this victory vanishes long before a second victory can be had. It is the rare team which can maintain the humility of the individual players long enough to create a dynasty.

"Basically, wisdom and history tell us that when we are most tempted to brag and bask in our own glory, that is when embracing humility is most important. If we wish to stay on the mountaintop for any length of time, it is only through the grace of others that we can do so. The grace of others is best attained through humility and through sharing what bounty we receive with those around us.

"That having been said, there is another equally dangerous problem with ego. Surrendering all sense of self-determination and self-reliance is just as harmful as an over-inflated ego. If we find ourselves in a valley, the worst thing we can do is to lay down and accept it. When we lay down, we tell the world that we quit, that we are defeated.

"People will invest their time and effort and even their money to help those who are striving or struggling, but they will rarely help those who have surrendered totally. No one wants to invest in a lost cause. If we find ourselves temporarily beaten by circumstance, it is vitally important for us to stand up and declare the battle to be far from over. We must let others know that we are not done fighting and that we are open to receiving help to renew our fight to get ahead.

"Managing our egos is a most challenging exercise, as the wisest course of action happens to be exactly the opposite of the natural reaction. When we succeed, the natural reaction is to celebrate and rejoice in our victory.

"While it is good to enjoy our accomplishments, we must remember that none of us succeeds alone and that the next victory is dependent on a whole new effort and set of actions and plans. This victory does not pre-ordain our next one. If we allow ego to prevent us from keeping up the same level of effort and from expressing the same humility, the next step in our journey may be a tumble down the mountain instead of up the next mountain.

"A healthy self-esteem allows us to be humble when we are doing well, and to be bold and confident when we are not doing so well. The key is to know the difference."

LESSON: When you are on the mountaintop, bow down low. When you are in the valley, stand tall.

Chapter Twenty-Two
The Million Dollar Baseball Card

This closing transaction marked the sale of the final home in the neighborhood they developed together. As they had agreed, Tommy and Ernie formed a partnership for this project that called for Tommy and his company to provide the financing and handle all the paperwork items like taxes, zoning issues, permits, and paying the subcontractors.

Ernie and his company oversaw the actual construction of the homes and made sure they were well-built, and they addressed any concerns that the new homeowners brought to their attention.

Although this project was, by far, the largest one they had completed together, they had been doing similar, but smaller things, for many years. Tommy helped Ernie finance his first few small remodeling jobs and often provided financing for his customers as well. Tommy was the partner with the pen and Ernie was the man with the hammer. Their relationship went all the way back to grade school and started around the same time that Tommy started learning from the Old Man next door.

The completion of this neighborhood represented a seven-figure profit for each of them. It took several years to complete and certainly involved a fair share of challenges. The factor that helped them get through the difficulties more than any other was that they trusted each other absolutely. They never worried about the motives of the other partner. If one told the other that something needed to be done, it was accepted and acted upon. They made mistakes, but they never lied or deceived one another.

As they were leaving the office where they signed the final papers and received their final checks, they stopped for a moment to reflect on what they had just achieved. The fact that they both came from similarly modest backgrounds was not lost on them. Tommy opened his folder and took out something he had been wanting to give to Ernie for a long time, and now seemed like the perfect time. He handed Ernie an old baseball card in a plastic sleeve. It was well-worn, the corners were rounded over, and the surface was heavily damaged. Ernie looked at it curiously for a moment, and then smiled broadly as he recognized the card. "What is this?" he asked. Tommy replied casually, "That my friend, is a million-dollar baseball card!"

Ernie knew the card, it was the card he had traded to Tommy in grade school many years ago.

Ernie was no expert on collectibles, but he knew enough to realize this particular card was not valuable in the least. It had some sentimental value, of course, but no real value. He turned it over in his hands and tried to figure out what Tommy meant by million-dollar card. He had heard many times over the years about the Old Man and his lessons and stories from Tommy. He sensed that he was about to hear another tale about the Old Man. He was right.

Tommy asked, "Do you remember when we agreed to that trade?" "Of course. It was when we became friends." Ernie answered.

"Well there was just a little bit more to that trade then you knew." Tommy replied.

Tommy explained, "Before we made that trade, I went to the Old Man to brag about what a great deal I had negotiated with you. I told him about how great this card was, and how I was getting it from you for another card that was worthless. I was quite proud of how well I had learned my lessons. Apparently, I had missed a lesson. The Old Man insisted that if the deal wasn't good for both of us, it wasn't a good deal at all. He told me that I had to be honest with you about the deal or I had to cancel it. He said that if I told you about your card being worth more, and you still wanted to do the deal, then it was fine. If you wanted to back out, I was supposed to let you do so without any complaining from me. Do you remember that?"

Ernie chuckled, "Yeah, I do. It made me think that you were a good guy for telling me that. Now, I know it was just the Old Man, after all! Yeah, I knew it was a bad deal, but I needed your card to complete a set I was working on, I had doubles of this card", shaking the battered card in his hand. "Plus, I was taught that a deal was a deal, and I wouldn't have backed out anyway."

Tommy continued, "When I came home and told the Old Man what happened, he was pleased, and he told me that you had 'integrity' and you had just taught it to me. He explained that integrity was doing what you agreed to do, even if it isn't in your favor. He praised you and told me to stay friends with you if I could, as having friends with integrity is something rare and valuable. That is why I always trusted you all these years, I never once had reason to doubt your integrity, and I tried to never give you reason to doubt mine. Now, look at us. We just cleared seven figures each. We provided good homes for over a hundred families. We provided a lot of construction work for dozens of workmen and paid a bunch of taxes. We did a lot of good, but we might not have been here today if not for that baseball card right there, that is why I called it the million-dollar baseball card."

Ernie was an emotional guy naturally, so this story told by his life-long friend had him leaking water from both eyes and trembling lightly. "Thank you for this, old friend. It means more to me than this check," he said patting his chest where the final check was in his pocket. "Well, not more! But almost!" Ernie shook his friend's hand and headed to his truck. Tommy couldn't wait to share with the Old Man how much Ernie had enjoyed the card and the story. Since the Old Man's diagnosis and dire prognosis, Tommy was eager to share with him stories that showed the far-reaching impacts of his lessons and stories. He wasn't sure how much longer he would have with his mentor, but he knew that there were now more days together behind them than in front of them for sure.

The Old Man's legacy in Tommy's life was undeniable. Tommy felt it important to show him how much his wisdom had affected others as well, through Tommy and indirectly through the people that Tommy did business with, and his family. Everything the Old Man taught him had a ripple effect, and Tommy's fondest wish for the Old Man before he passed was for him to get a glimpse of the good that came from his wisdom and his willingness to share it freely. He also wanted to allow his teacher every opportunity to continue sharing until the last moment, as he knew the Old Man would want.

LESSON: Integrity is everything. Do what you say and do not cheat anyone, you only cheat yourself if you do.

CHAPTER TWENTY-THREE
Priorities

Although their high school dating years had been occasionally rocky and even tumultuous, Tommy and Theresa's relationship survived and flourished past high school. A few years afterwards, they were married in a modest ceremony. It was attended by a few friends and family members, including, of course, the Old Man. Following the Old Man's advice, they soon started a business together and made plans for starting a family.

Their home improvement business was doing well. In just a few years, they had built up a solid list of clients and a well-deserved reputation for quality work at a reasonable price. Tommy and Theresa made a great team. They complimented each other well. She was a gregarious people person, and Tommy had a talent for getting jobs done on time and under budget, even when they encountered unexpected challenges.

They were in the middle of an ambitious expansion plan. They were not only expanding their service area geographically, they were also expanding the menu of services they were offering to their clients.

However, the arrival of their twins forced Theresa to withdraw almost completely from the business activities, as newborn twins were a full-time job to say the least. Her absence was causing Tommy to have to work a lot more hours to keep their expansion plans on track. With the twins' arrival, Tommy was more determined than ever to see the plans through. He had calculated that after the expansion, his income would double in four years or so.

Being home a lot less than usual was causing Tommy and Theresa to have some issues. There were several heated 'discussions' over Tommy's work schedule. Tommy was having difficulty explaining to Theresa the need for him to work so hard, especially now with the expansion underway. He called the Old Man, hoping he could help Tommy with one of his old stories or lessons to show Theresa what he wanted her to accept.

That was the plan, anyway. Like most plans, however, it went off the rails almost immediately. Tommy spent an hour talking without interruption. The Old Man sat quietly as Tommy laid out for him all the details of the expansion, how much more money it would bring in, and how much more quickly Tommy would be able to reach some of his investing goals with the extra income.

He described, in great detail, the contents of their arguments and had no trouble pinpointing exactly why Theresa was wrong to complain about how much he was working.

When Tommy finally stopped talking long enough to catch his breath and try to gauge the Old Man's reaction to everything he'd laid out, he was surprised to see that the Old Man was misty eyed and clearly saddened by Tommy's troubles. An emotional reaction like this was rare for the Old Man, and Tommy was starting to regret bringing his personal problems to him.

"Tommy, I owe you an apology. Much of this situation is my fault. I was so intent on making sure you didn't repeat some of my mistakes and making sure you were preparing for your future, I failed to help you prepare for the present.

"Because I had no children of my own, I may have neglected to include them in my life lessons, though they are obviously very important. I failed you, and I will try to help you as much as I can to fix this.

"The first thing I will tell you to help you out is that you are wrong. Theresa is right, and you are wrong. I will take some of the blame for you being wrong, but you are wrong nonetheless.

"Tommy, how much did you make the year before you began the expansion?" the Old Man asked.

Tommy told him the figure, which was several times more than the average income in their state. The Old Man already knew the number because he helped Tommy with his tax strategies, but he needed Tommy to hear himself say the number out loud.

"Could you and Theresa and the boys survive on that much, at least for a few years?" the Old Man continued.

"Well, I guess we could survive, but we wouldn't really move ahead any." Tommy replied.

"In order to maintain your previous income, would you have to work as hard as you are working now?"

Tommy answered, "No, I guess not. Many of my guys are getting better and more experienced. I could let them do more without me being there. I could work a few hours less per day."

The Old Man explained, "Tommy, while your ultimate plan is to achieve total time freedom for the future, having a measure of time freedom right now is also valuable. Your wife and your boys need you right now, and any time freedom you achieve in the future cannot be used retroactively.

"You can never come back in time to participate in these first few years. Once these years pass, they are gone forever, and they are too precious and important to miss. You can make plenty of money to support your family because you have managed to keep your expenses reasonable and have some money invested already for emergencies and as a cushion.

"The boys will form their own ideas about money and prosperity based on what they observe at home, long before they are old enough for actual lessons from you. They will know that their father was always there and that they could afford to go places and do things together as a family.

"They will know that their father worked hard, but that work wasn't his biggest priority, they were. By being there for your children's formative years, you are not only helping them to develop healthy ideas about family, they are developing a healthy attitude towards work and prosperity as well.

"Tommy, being home for your family will pay dividends that far outweigh the few dollars you won't make now. Once the boys are old enough to be in school all day, you and Theresa can both work together again and soon make up any lost time and income. Being together for the boys will make you stronger as a couple and as business partners.

"Once the boys are old enough to participate, their view of the family business will not be one of envy because the business kept their father away. Their attitude will be that the family business gave their father the freedom to be home with them, which is something that not all families enjoy.

"It is easy to get caught up in our work and forget why we work so hard in the first place. If our work ruins our family, why are we working in the first place? What are we fighting for, if not a strong family unit? Can we have a strong family unit if one parent is missing more than necessary? The whole point of striving for success is to achieve some measure of time freedom, but if everything we love is destroyed before we use some of that freedom, it will seem empty later when we finally get there."

The Old Man helped Tommy to understand that he was only as successful in business as he was in strengthening his family. Achieving great wealth is an empty victory if all else is lost in the process. Better to get only halfway there with your family happy, healthy, and intact than to get all the way there alone and with your family broken. Keep your priorities straight and everything else will fall in place as it should.

LESSON: Family first; or what is the point of striving?
Getting there alone is not getting there at all.

CHAPTER TWENTY-FOUR
Hero or Villain

It was the twins' birthday and the Old Man was enjoying his time at Tommy's house. The boys were playing in the pool, Theresa and Tommy's mother Norah were preparing a salad in the kitchen, and Tommy was busy ruining their steaks on the barbecue by the back porch. The Old Man was just observing, and occasionally needling Tommy for overcooking perfectly good steaks.

Norah's medical transportation business had flourished with some guidance from the Old Man, but he was always quick to deflect taking any credit for her success. She had done all the hard work involved. He had simply pointed her in the right direction from time to time. She was currently negotiating the purchase of a similar business operating in the next town that would nearly double the size of her business when completed.

Tommy and Theresa's business was doing well also. The company they owned was now the leading home improvement company in town, they offered many services and had built a solid base of referrals which kept them busy even when other businesses struggled. The Old Man took pride in the prosperity his teaching had inspired here, but he couldn't help but wonder how many more people he could have helped if he had proffered his lessons more intentionally over the years.

The Old Man enjoyed these gatherings, these people had become his family, in many ways, his first such family. He had been happily married for many years, but never had children or grandchildren of his own. He felt both a feeling of satisfaction and a measure of regret for not having experienced this before now.

Once the steaks were finished, Tommy called the boys to the table and Theresa brought the green salad and the potato salad from inside. They had made it a point to include the Old Man in all their family gatherings and he really felt like a part of the family. He often felt like he was living vicariously through Tommy, but he was not uncomfortable with the feeling. He felt like his mentorship had helped Tommy get where he was, so he took a lot of pride and joy while he was with the family.

As they all sat down to eat, the Old Man noticed that Tommy seemed happy, but just a little bit distracted. Once they were finished eating, and the boys were clearing the table, the Old Man asked Tommy what was bugging him. Tommy didn't seem surprised that the Old Man had caught onto his distraction.

"It's just a little thing with a customer that I am struggling with, nothing major, just something new for me," Tommy answered.

"Well, don't keep an old man in suspense, tell me all about it."

"A few years ago, my crew and I installed some gutters on a house. We did a good job and we always give a lifetime warranty with our work. Yesterday, the customer called and said a section of his gutter was sagging and asked me to come by and fix it. Since we like to back up our work, I agreed and went by with my crew.

"When I got there, I immediately realized that the problem wasn't anything we had done wrong with the installation, but instead was caused by the customer himself failing to clean his gutters. There was a tennis ball totally blocking the downspout so that no water could escape the gutters. This caused the water to gather in the gutters and eventually the weight caused it to sag," Tommy explained.

"Ok, so what is your dilemma?" the Old Man asked.

"Well, we went ahead and fixed the gutter. We replaced the damage section and removed the obstructions. My issue is, since this was not our fault, why should I not charge the customer to fix it? He seemed to think it was a warranty issue, but it clearly wasn't."

"How much did it cost you to change the gutter?" "About a hundred bucks, I guess." answered Tommy.

"It wasn't your fault, right? Not your problem? The answer is obvious, isn't it?' suggested the Old Man.

"Yeah, I guess so, I will bill him for the work." Tommy concluded.

"What? No, you idiot! Haven't you learned anything yet?" the Old Man smiled as he enjoyed watching Tommy squirm a bit. The Old Man had come for some nice family time and some birthday cake, but he was going to have to earn his meal today with one more lesson for his student.

"Tommy, listen closely. Tomorrow, and for a few weeks or months, every time a discussion comes up about gutters, or home improvement projects, or contractors, that customer is going to relate this story as his contribution to the conversation.

"This is the story he will tell everyone who will listen. The question is: Do you want to be the villain or the hero in his story, repeated many times over?"

Tommy looked confused still, so the Old Man continued. He is going to tell one of two possible different versions of this story. In one version, he had a problem with his gutters he bought from you with a lifetime warranty. When he called you, you came right out and blamed him for the problem and charged him to fix the gutters that were supposed to be under warranty."

Tommy interrupted, "But that isn't really fair."

"Do you think he is going to tell all his friends that he failed to clean his gutters and caused them to fail? Even if he believes you when you explain it to him, do you know for a fact that he will relate the story that way to all of his friends and family and co-workers?"

Tommy admitted quietly, "I guess not."

"The other version he could tell is how he had a problem with his gutters and you came out right away and fixed them with no fuss or complaining. Which version would be better for you and your business in the long run?" the Old Man asked.

"Of course, the second version would be better for me." Tommy answered.

"OK, so you would prefer the 'hero' version over the 'villain' version? Good choice. The cost of that version is about one hundred dollars. You can be the hero for a hundred dollars, or you can keep the money and be the villain. It is that simple, really."

Tommy nodded in agreement, but the Old Man wanted to make a small clarification and a distinction so that Tommy wouldn't mistakenly apply the same logic to every situation.

"Tommy, have you ever heard the saying, 'the customer is always right'?" Tommy said he had. "Well, that is nonsense. Sometimes the customer is dead wrong, and sometimes you must have the courage to tell them so right to their face. It isn't easy to do sometimes, but you will know when this applies.

"Sometimes the customer wants you to do something you simply cannot or should not do. Sometimes they want you to do something that will harm them or the quality of your work or they will want you to do something unethical or even illegal. Sometimes they will want you to do something for free or so cheap that it hurts your business.

"There are many times when the customer is wrong. There are times when you must stand up to them. This is NOT one of those times. Gently explain to the customer what you found, if he is ethical, he will offer to pay you. Gently refuse the money and tell him everyone gets one 'freebie' and this is his. Thank him for his business and go on your way."

Tommy was in the middle of thanking the Old Man for his unscheduled lesson when Theresa, Norah, and the boys emerged with the birthday cake and the candles. Theresa set the cake down and lit the candles. The Old Man sang the happy birthday song along with Tommy, Theresa, and Norah. For just a moment, he regretted not having ever sang this same song to kids of his own, but he sure was enjoying it now. "The oldest person at the party gets the first piece of cake, don't you know that?" he said as he rose to grab a plate and a fork. He was already looking forward to next year's party.

LESSON: Whenever possible, be the hero in someone's story, and try to never be the villain!

CHAPTER TWENTY-FIVE
St. Catherine's Cathedral

Nowadays, Tommy was so busy with his family and growing business, he found it difficult to find the time to stop in to see him, even though he always left the Old Man feeling wiser and wealthier than when he arrived.

Tommy had done as the Old Man instructed, he had made learning a mainstay of his daily routine, just like brushing his teeth and showering. Every day he devoted thirty minutes of his time to reading. With his schedule, he rarely found time to read more than thirty minutes, but he was proud that it had been a long time since he had missed a reading session.

As he always did before he visited the Old Man, Tommy was mentally running through his checklist like a student checking his notes before a big test. He knew the Old Man would grill him as he always had.

Tommy was excited to see his mentor, but he was also slightly nervous for this visit. He had seemingly reached a plateau, but it felt different from previous plateaus. It had a more "dead end" feel to it. He was making more money than most people would consider "enough," and his life was nearly perfect to any casual observer.

Yet, Tommy had felt for many months now that something was profoundly wrong. He was worried both about the judgment of the Old Man and the possibility that he had just reached the limits of his potential and there would be nothing the Old Man could do about it.

Tommy was certain the Old Man had left no stone unturned in his education. The last several times he had encountered problems, he had been able to sift through the Old Man's lessons etched in his mind and come up with a solution. Not this time though, Tommy was stuck, and it terrified him.

Tommy wasn't scared of not making more money, he had as much as he needed already.

Tommy was afraid of living a life where forward progress and personal growth were absent. To him, that would indeed be a life not worth living, a life of "quiet desperation," as a wise man once phrased it.

All his adult life so far, Tommy had regularly received words of praise and respect for his achievements from his family, friends, and business associates. As nice as this was, Tommy's real satisfaction came when the Old Man praised him. His praise was much harder to come by, so it meant that much more to him.

Tommy could bear losing status among his friends if his income dropped or stalled, but if the Old Man thought he had stopped growing it would be devastating to Tommy. This was why he had delayed sharing his latest challenge with the Old Man until now, when he felt he had no other option.

As he pulled into the Old Man's driveway, he resolved to do as he always had been taught to do, he would just lay it out there and handle whatever came.

He knocked twice loudly, and then let himself in. The Old Man had admonished him too often for making him get up to open the door for someone so much younger than himself.

The Old Man was in his usual spot, scribbling busily in his notebook. When Tommy entered the room, the Old Man put his pen down and closed his notebook to give Tommy his full attention.

Tommy noticed that the Old Man's body seemed a bit smaller, but his eyes shone even brighter than ever which countered the effect and left him looking as energetic and sharp as he ever did.

They spent a few minutes catching up and exchanging the niceties that old friends exchange after a long separation.

"Spit it out, Tommy. I know this isn't a social visit. What troubles you?" the Old Man was nothing if not predictable.

Tommy knew better than to be coy with the Old Man, so he blurted out, "I feel like I have gone as far as I can, and it scares the heck out of me." Tommy managed a calm appearance outwardly, but internally, he was tying himself in knots wondering how the Old Man would react.

After a brief pause, the Old Man replied softly, "Tell me more."

Tommy briefly explained how his income and financial picture were strong enough, but they had remained largely unchanged for several years. "I don't need more money, but I have some good ideas, big ones, that I would like to pursue, and they would need funding on a scale larger than I could provide now. I know I would be fine financially if I stayed where I am now, but I feel like there are lots of people I could help that might not be helped if I fail to move forward and that is what really bothers me."

The Old Man listened intently and waited for a few moments to make sure Tommy had finished his thoughts. Then he got up and beckoned for Tommy to follow him into the hallway. He pointed to a picture hanging there. Tommy had passed the picture hundreds of times but had never stopped to look at it closely.

It was not one of those pictures that grabs your attention. It was a picture of a huge set of stairs with a church at the top. The church itself was barely visible because the stairs seemed to be the focus of the photographer.

The Old Man asked as he tapped the photo with his finger, "What do you see?" Tommy quipped, "Proof that you are terrible at taking pictures?"

The Old Man didn't even crack a smile and pointed again. "Look closer," he commanded.

Tommy quickly wiped the smirk from his face and looked at the picture again, but for the first time, if that makes any sense. "I see stairs, lots and lots of stairs."

"What else do you see? Tell me everything you see in that picture."

"I see lots of stairs leading up to a large church. There are a lot of people at the bottom of the stairs. There are a few people climbing, and a few people at the top. There is one man who is coming down the stairs. There is also a lot of grass on either side of the stairs."

"Better. Now we are getting somewhere. Now describe the stairs in more detail," the Old Man insisted.

Tommy knew better than to question the request and simply obeyed. "The stairs are short, but deep in depth. There is a landing after every ten stairs or so. They are wide enough for several people to climb them, side by side with no problem."

"Excellent, Tommy. Now, tell me more precisely what is vexing you."

Tommy knew this question was coming and he was prepared for it. He told the Old Man how diligent he had been about reading every day. He explained how he had been setting goals and failing to reach them. He knew all the protocols for goal setting and achieving, he had read all the books and they all had chapters on goals.

They varied somewhat, but they had common elements that made lots of sense to him and had presumably worked well for the authors themselves and others. He told the Old Man how he had written down his goals. He had made them audacious enough to inspire him.

He read them aloud every morning and every evening. He always kept them close by. He even announced his goals to his family and friends. He declared them as already achieved with his positive affirmations. He had followed the directions to the letter but had not achieved a significant goal in quite some time.

The Old Man listened patiently. He pointed to the picture again. "That church at the top of these stairs is St. Catherine's Cathedral in Montreal. It is one of the most magnificent cathedrals in the world.

"The beauty of the inside of this cathedral is impossible to describe with only words. I am not a religious man. But standing in that cathedral could only be described as a religious experience. I had not experienced such a profound sense of awe and wonder in my entire life, and I have not since, and I took that photo several decades ago."

Tommy couldn't resist, "Then why the heck didn't you take a picture of the inside instead of the stupid stairs?"

The Old Man laughed and explained, "For one thing, a picture could never convey the splendor of that cathedral adequately, especially a photo taken by someone, as you rightly noted, who is as bad a photographer as myself. For another thing, I paid dearly for that view by climbing those stairs in the summer heat. Let everyone else climb the stairs themselves if they want the experience. I can only tell them that the climb is worth the effort. I can't make them climb the stairs."

He continued, "I focused on the stairs because I was struck by all the life lessons contained and illustrated in that simple set of stairs. I could write an entire book just on those stairs and the wisdom they embody. See this group gathered at the bottom? When I arrived, I asked them how they had enjoyed the cathedral.

"They told me that they had heard how awesome it was, but no one had told them about the stairs. They had decided that the experience wasn't worth the climb. You can't see it in the photo, but one of them was looking up at the cathedral with binoculars!"

The Old Man turned to Tommy to make sure he had his full attention. "Those people represent all the people in the world who say they want to experience life to the fullest, but are not willing to pay the price, so they look at the better things from a distance and complain about how unfair it is that the better things are so hard to reach.

"Of course, that means that the cathedral itself represents the more exquisite things and experiences that life has to offer all of us," he added.

"What about the people on the steps?" Tommy asked. The Old Man now had not only his attention, but his interest. Tommy was starting to get the picture- literally!

"Those are the people that are somewhere on their journey. Some will make it to the top, and some will turn around midway like this guy here." He pointed to the one man descending the stairs.

Tommy could almost make out his dejection, even from a distance. "Notice how many more people there are at the bottom than the top. This means the higher you go, the less competition there is, because not many are willing to pay the cost."

Tommy was enjoying the lesson, but he was ready to hear the Old Man address his problem specifically. The Old Man sensed Tommy's restlessness and told him, "Now, let's use this old picture to solve your problem. Go get that goal list from your car and let's have a look at it."

Tommy half walked, half jogged to his car to retrieve his list. He had not one clue what the Old Man was going to tell him, but he felt better already. The Old Man seemed fully engaged now, and Tommy knew that meant he would be able to help.

When he returned, he handed the list to the Old Man. The Old Man scanned the list for about one half of a second and handed it back. He had seen exactly what he expected to see. He motioned to the picture one more time.

"If you were right here, looking up at the cathedral, knowing how magnificent it was to behold, what would you do?" the Old Man asked.

"I would climb those stairs in record time!" Tommy answered quickly. "What if I removed every other stair?" the Old Man asked.

"That would certainly make it harder, but I would still find a way."

"What if there were only the bottom stair and the top stair? What if there were no stairs between?" the Old Man smirked as he looked at Tommy.

"Now that is ridiculous, I obviously couldn't climb stairs that don't exist!" Tommy complained.

The Old Man pointed at the paper in Tommy's left hand. "Show me your list again." Tommy obeyed, now realizing where the Old Man was going. The Old Man pointed at the top item on the list. It read "I earn two million dollars per year."

"Where are the stairs?"

Tommy was struck both by the depth of the wisdom and the fact that it was so simple. "So, you are saying that the stairs represent increments of income, and I am trying to skip too many stairs at once." Tommy was relieved and ready to go home and begin to apply this lesson right away.

"Close, but not quite. You see the stairs really represent levels of your personal growth.

When your personal growth level rises high enough, the income will follow. You need to grow more if you want to earn more. Right now, you earn exactly what you deserve to earn based on the person you are, maybe even a little more." He smiled at his student.

"Reading is important. But try some other things. Go to some seminars. Take some classes. Think about alternative sources of income like royalties, licensing fees, dividends, etc. You have made a lot of money with your one business, now it is time to expand into other businesses and projects.

"Decide what interests you and find someone already doing it well. Read their books, try to meet them, ask them questions. Just be prepared to fail at first, because as you know, failure almost always precedes growth."

LESSON: Your income is not just a random figure, it reflects the market value of your current level of personal growth. If you want to make more, you must become more!

CHAPTER TWENTY-SIX
True Prosperity

It had been several weeks since the Old Man had helped Tommy solve his goal-setting and achieving problem using the stairs of St. Catherine's as a learning tool. He had not heard from Tommy since, so he assumed he was hard at work doing what he had encouraged him to do.

That notion changed quickly when Tommy's wife, Theresa, called him. He had met her many times over the years. He found her to be quite bright and enjoyed quite a few casual, but pleasant, conversations with her. She was quite a bit more sociable than himself, but she was a perfect match for Tommy as far as he could tell. He barely recognized her voice over the phone. She was clearly upset and asked to see the Old Man without Tommy.

Fearing the worst, that something had happened to Tommy, he quickly agreed and asked her to come right over. When she arrived, the Old Man opened the door for her and hung her jacket on the stand in the hallway.

He led her into the living room and guided her to Tommy's usual spot on the couch. He sat next to her, and she began talking immediately. Apparently, Tommy had shared with her the Old Man's aversion to small talk and he was grateful for that, now more than ever.

"I am worried about Tommy," she said, her voice cracking with emotion. "Is he sick, did something happen?" asked the Old Man

"No, not exactly", she answered. The Old Man was relieved somewhat, but still concerned. He waited for her to continue. She did. "After his last visit with you, Tommy changed. He became more focused, almost obsessed with making more money. I know that doesn't sound like a bad thing to you, but I fear Tommy is becoming, well, greedy."

The word always hit the Old Man like a punch in the gut no matter how many times he heard it. To him, it was the worst insult anyone could throw at him. Hearing it thrown at Tommy was doubly injurious to him. He had been vigilant to steer Tommy away from the ugliness of greed and instead towards true prosperity, which he considered to be the opposite of greed.

"Why do you think it is greed that drives him?" the Old Man asked gently.

"What else could it be?" she asked. "We already have so much. We couldn't spend our money in a lifetime. We don't need a bigger house. We don't need another zero in our bank account. We don't need more money! We have already come so far from where we began, how much is enough?"

The Old Man sighed. He was relieved. He knew what the problem was, and it wasn't greed at all. Theresa didn't have the advantage of Tommy's many lessons for the Old Man to refer to, so he chose to use the lesson that had inspired Tommy to explain to his wife what was truly driving Tommy. "Do me a favor, Theresa, go into the hallway and take the picture of the cathedral down and bring it here."

She did as he asked. She handed the picture to him and sat back down on the couch next to him. He briefly explained to her what the stairs represented and what the cathedral itself represented. Then he added a distinction that he hadn't yet used with Tommy because he felt that Tommy had already made the distinction instinctively without the Old Man's help. He just hadn't been able to express it to Theresa because he wasn't consciously aware of what was driving him.

But the Old Man knew. He pointed to a spot in the picture near the top of the stairs. "This point here, this is where you and Tommy are right now. You have more than most people, and considering where you started, it is quite impressive. From here, you can see through the front door of the cathedral.

"You can catch a glimpse of the sanctuary inside. You can see some of the beauty and splendor, but you cannot see all of it and you cannot feel it. The inside, the sanctuary, represents true prosperity, the highest level of prosperity attainable.

"I told Tommy that standing in that sanctuary could only be described as a religious experience. What I meant by that is that the feeling would be so profound and so deeply moving, that your first instinct is to share it with other people."

The Old Man went on to share with Theresa some of the ideas that Tommy had shared with him. Tommy and Theresa already wrote checks to several charities every year. This was not charity, this was something different. Tommy wanted to help other people see the sanctuary for themselves.

Tommy had decided that he wanted to fund and teach a personal finance class at a community center. He wanted to teach folks about things like credit, investing, and starting a business. He wanted to fund scholarships for local high school students to go to college if they had no other means of paying for it.

He wanted to establish a fund to help local people start businesses and to help existing businesses to expand. He wanted to fund a job training program to help folks update their skills.

Tommy and Theresa had enough money for themselves, but to do these other things, it would take substantially more money, and that would require growing beyond who they were now.

By this time, Theresa's eyes were wet again. The Old Man sensed, though, that these were happy tears, not sad ones. "I had no idea he wanted to do all those things. We had talked about some of them, but I didn't know how important they were to him. What do I do now, how do I help?"

"Oh, that's easy," said the Old Man. "Take his hand in yours and tell him, 'I am with you, I've got your back.'"

LESSON: Greed is wanting more for yourself.
True prosperity is wanting more for others.

Chapter Twenty-Seven
The Rodeo

The only person who had less interest than Tommy in going to a rodeo on a hot summer day was the Old Man. Yet, here they were, sweating and feigning interest in a sport that neither of them understood in the least. Even less than they understood the event itself did they understand the fervent enthusiasm of the participants and most of the crowd.

The plain truth was, Theresa had talked Tommy into going and Tommy had talked the Old Man into it. The Old Man understood how important it was for Tommy to support her interests and he demonstrated that by showing his support for Tommy by joining them and the boys on this excursion.

Tommy was a married man with children now, and his lessons had become fewer and farther between. Tommy now often made observations on his own that impressed the Old Man. He sometimes helped him see things from a different perspective and that made him even more proud than how well Tommy learned his lessons. Tommy often was the teacher, and today would be one of those times.

Towards the end of the rodeo, an event caught the Old Man's genuine interest. He saw an opportunity to illustrate a concept that he felt Tommy and his family would find helpful. A tiny girl, no more than ten years old, was "showing" a gigantic show horse that was so much bigger than she that it was comical.

The crowd, of course, loved her. She paraded the huge beast around and gave commands in a manner that would make a seasoned combat general proud. She was in total command of the huge creature, though he obviously could have tossed her like a dishrag at any moment. While the crowd and even Tommy and his family were impressed by the small girl, the Old Man saw something else entirely.

"That right there," he gestured towards the girl in the center of the ring, is a perfect illustration of why so many people end up so broke and miserable in a country almost defined by prosperity and the pursuit of happiness."

Tommy laughed out loud. "You sure have a way of raining on any parade, don't you?" He said jokingly. "But please, do tell. Please explain how you got all that from watching this cute kid and her horse." By now, Theresa and the boys had turned their attention to the exchange between Tommy and the Old Man.

The girl was walking her horse back to the gate she had emerged from, so this conversation right here became the main show for them. They weren't sure, but it seemed that Tommy was almost challenging the Old Man. They had never seen any hint of that before, so they were fixated.

"What I see there is an amazing and powerful creature held back by a force so much weaker than itself, and that is a tragedy. For me, that horse represents the inherent strength and creativity and potential in all people. The little girl and the thin rope she controls the creature with, represent the past failures and faulty concepts that so many good people allow to hold them back from their destiny, though they are so much more powerful than they realize. They could break free of their self-made limitations if they were aware of their inner strength and the relative weakness of what holds them back.

"The problem is that the failures and faulty concepts were implanted in them before they were so strong. They don't know how powerful they have become. They haven't noticed how the rope and the small child holding it have lost their relative strength over time. They never noticed, like the elephant held in place by the tiny stake in the ground." explained the Old Man.

"Elephant and a stake?" asked Theresa.

Tommy knew this story, but Theresa had not heard it, so the Old Man continued, "Yes, when a baby elephant is born into the circus, the trainers use a small wooden stake hammered into the ground and tie the elephant to it to keep it from wandering off. At first, the small elephant pulls against the stake to no avail. He isn't strong enough to pull it from the ground. After a short while, he stops trying. He accepts his fate.

"So deeply does he accept it, that when he grows bigger and stronger, he doesn't bother even trying, though the stake has remained small and he has grown much stronger. Sadly, this is exactly what happens to so many people. Many people never even bother trying to pull against the stake because they were told by their parents not to bother, the stake was too strong.

"They were taught to be content to live within the range of the rope they were born with.

Some try a few small tugs, like starting a small business. They fail once or twice, and they quit. They accept that the rope and the stake are too strong for them. Then they resign themselves to a life of mediocrity and struggle, though they become stronger over time. To me this is a great tragedy."

Tommy spoke up. "That is definitely an important lesson. Thank you for that. However, I saw something a little different in that same scene. What I saw was a person who was small in stature take command over something that seemed much stronger than herself because she understood the nature of the beast himself. She had the knowledge, the confidence, and desire to overcome the beast's apparently insurmountable size.

"She didn't control it with brute force: she controlled it with ability. To me, the horse represented all the potential pitfalls that investing and the pursuit of prosperity entail. A person without the education, confidence, and desire to conquer the problems and challenges would surely be overpowered by them.

"The little girl overcame them instead with preparation and character, though she be but little in size. To me, this is a lesson in the strength of ability over natural advantage," Tommy explained.

Theresa and the boys hesitated to respond. They were waiting for the Old Man's reaction. He sat quietly for a moment. Then he slowly grinned, eventually flashing a broad smile and laughed out loud. "Excellent, Tommy. Maybe I haven't been wasting my time all these years after all!"

Theresa and the boys smiled, and they all started gathering their things to head back to the parking lot to go home, since the little girl's demonstration was the last of the day and the rest of the crowd had already left, leaving them as the last to leave the rodeo.

The conversation continued as they drove home. "How would you summarize these observations, Tommy?" asked the Old Man.

Tommy was quiet for a minute then he said, "I guess the truth is so many people are held back by forces they imagine to be much stronger than they really are, and that with some education, confidence, and desire, people are capable of overcoming much larger obstacles than they realize. They need more knowledge, not necessarily more 'muscle.'"

"Now be more specific, Tommy. How does that apply in real-life terms?" The Old Man asked.

"I think many people do not start businesses because they imagine the process to be complicated and difficult and expensive. Yet small children often start business like I did in school selling gum and candy to the other kids.

"They see huge international conglomerates and they get scared, but a business can normally be started fairly easily if the idea is sound. Also, I think so many folks never invest because they are afraid of the investing world, they are overly afraid of losing money, so they never make any. If they would simply learn the terms and the language of investing, they would be relieved to realize that the basics of investing are quite simple once you learn the terms involved.

"Let me add one more distinction" the Old Man volunteered as they pulled into Tommy's driveway. "People need to be taught to never stop pulling on that small wooden stake, even if it didn't break before. Every time they read a book or learn something new, or try something new, their strength increases and their chance of breaking free gets better."

LESSON: Most of what holds us back is either imaginary or simply a shadow of a problem that passed a long time ago.

CHAPTER TWENTY-EIGHT
A Hundred Pennies

The first few times that the Old Man had visited Tommy's new house, he was not quite comfortable. His own house had never known the level of noise and activity that were commonplace at Tommy's house. Between the twins, Theresa, and Tommy himself, there was a lot going on there all the time.

Tommy's house was impressive. It wasn't ostentatious by any standard, and wouldn't qualify as a mansion by any measure, but it was well-built and well-appointed. It sat on a large lot with huge swaths of grass, that Tommy kept perfectly manicured. There was a small patch of woods at the rear of the lot where the boys often rode their bikes and played. The Old Man couldn't help but notice that Tommy's pool was similar in style to his own, but just a little bit bigger.

Over time, though, his visits became easier for him as he focused on watching how happy Tommy was, and how much his family loved him back. It warmed the Old Man's heart to think that he had played a role in how well Tommy was doing.

He had become like a grandfather to the twins and Theresa often confided in him when she wanted to surprise Tommy with some sort of treat, as Tommy was not prone to rewarding himself for his work. The Old Man was looking forward to this visit, although Tommy's tone on the phone concerned him somewhat.

When he drove up the long driveway, he noticed right away that something was different. Something felt off. The grass that was usually perfect looked like, well, everyone else's lawn, needing to be cut soon. As he walked around to the back door that led into the kitchen area, he noticed a few leaves in the pool. Again, this wasn't any worse than everybody else's pool, but it was notable here.

Theresa saw him approaching and opened the door before he could knock. She embraced him warmly as she always did, but the Old Man was sure she hugged him a little tighter and a little longer than she normally did.

The Old Man was still getting used to Theresa's non-verbal communication abilities, but she did remind him of his late wife in that regard. Millie could speak a "book with a look," as he used to tell her, and so could Theresa.

"He is up in his office. Go on up. I will bring you a cup of coffee," she said quietly.

As the Old Man climbed the stairs, he noticed that the handrail had just a tiny wiggle to it and the carpet on the stairs seemed more worn that the last time he was on those stairs. As he entered Tommy's office at the top of the stairs, he felt like he had reached the end of the trail of bread crumbs at last.

Tommy's desk surface was no longer visible. The wastebasket was overflowing, and Tommy flinched when the Old Man greeted him. Tommy had been so engrossed in the papers in front of him, he hadn't seen the Old Man approaching. He set his hand on Tommy's shoulder to keep him from getting up and looked around the room once more before clearing a stack of papers off the chair next to the desk and sitting down.

Theresa knocked on the open door and entered with a tray holding two cups of coffee and sugar and cream, complete with spoons and a few cookies. She placed the tray on a table behind the men and quietly left the room, closing the door when she went back downstairs to see what kind of trouble the twins were getting into.

The Old Man didn't have to pry anything out of Tommy this time. "I am at my wits' end. I want to do so many more things, but I just can't find the time to pursue anything else.

"Between the boys and Theresa, doing all this paperwork, running the installation crew all day, collecting rents from the duplexes, making repairs, cutting the grass, and trying to find a few minutes to exercise and read, I am just plumb out of time. I feel maxed out, and I hate the feeling. I feel like I am doing a lot of things, but none of them well," he blurted out.

The Old Man had hit this same wall himself many years before, and his own mentor had a gift for making his lessons easy to understand, yet powerful. He decided to teach Tommy the same lesson that he had learned a few decades before.

"Tommy, do you have a change jar around here somewhere?" asked the Old Man.

Confused, but much too smart to express it out loud, he answered, "In the kitchen downstairs."

"Come on, let's go down there for a minute. Grab the coffee. I want to share an old lesson directly from the real Old Man with you."

Tommy was curious, as the Old Man rarely invoked his mentor. He knew this lesson would be light on technical terms, yet profound.

When they got to the kitchen, the Old Man cleared off the kitchen table as Tommy retrieved the change jar from under a side table near the couch. Theresa and the boys had gathered around to see what was going on. They weren't sure what the Old Man was going to do, but they knew the Old Man was one of only a few people Tommy looked up to, so they knew whatever this was, it was important.

The Old Man dumped out the jar onto the table. He asked the boys to separate the pennies from the rest of the change. They were excited to help and made short work of the task. Once only pennies remained, he asked them to count out one hundred pennies and return the rest to the jar along with the nickels, dimes, and quarters.

Once there were only the one hundred pennies remaining, he spread them out in a large circle in the middle of the table. He explained, "Tommy, this pile of pennies represents you. They represent all your time, your attention, your thoughts and your personal effort. This is everything you have to give."

He counted out twenty pennies and pushed it to one side. "This pile represents Theresa and the boys." Theresa and the twins both looked at him a bit sideways because they thought their pile should be bigger, but they didn't dare interrupt the lesson.

He counted out twenty more pennies and set them aside, separate from the first pile. "This represents you leading your installation crew every day." He repeated the process. "This pile represents the time you spend collecting rents and performing maintenance on the duplexes," he counted out another twenty pennies. "This pile represents the time you spend doing paperwork for the business and the rental properties." He counted out 19 of the remaining twenty pennies and set it aside. "This pile represents the time you spend cutting grass, taking care of the pool and fixing handrails here." There remained a single penny in the middle. "And this lonely little fellow here, Tommy, is what you have left over to take care of yourself and learn, and read, and make plans to move forward with your life."

Tommy knew that he was stretched too thin but seeing it in such stark and obvious terms was eye-opening for him and Theresa. The boys were still looking at their skimpy pile, hoping there was more to this lesson.

"Okay, I see what you are telling me, but what can I do? I can't close my business, I can't give up the rental properties, I can't let the grass grow forever, and I certainly can't get rid of these guys!" gesturing towards the twins and Theresa.

"How is Phillip coming along?" asked the Old Man, referring to the man who was Tommy's most senior crew member.

"Honestly, he is better than I am. It has been a long time since I taught him anything he didn't already know," Tommy answered.

"Excellent. That is what I suspected. Starting Monday morning, let Phillip lead the crew on the job. Let him hire a helper so he won't be short-handed, but you stay home. You will have to pay him more, but," the Old Man pushed one of the twenty penny piles back into the middle of the table.

"As soon as you have Phillip set up and going, call this guy," he said as he handed Tommy a business card from his wallet. "He is the best property manager I know. He will screen tenants, collect deposits and rents. He will handle maintenance and even keep records for the duplexes. He charges a percentage, but he is worth several times what he charges." The Old Man then pushed another pile back into the middle of the table.

"After you meet with the property manager and turn the keys to the duplexes over to him, ask Theresa to get on the internet to look for a landscaper and a pool maintenance company to take care of some of the things around here for you. Again, this will cost a few bucks, but it will be well worth it.

"Finally, call this woman." He reached into his wallet once again. "She is the best CPA I know. She can set you up with a bookkeeper to help with your paperwork, and she will help you with your tax strategy as well."

He pushed another pile of pennies back to the middle of the table. "Now what?" Tommy sensed that this lesson wasn't over yet.

The Old Man divided the now quite large pile of pennies roughly in half and pushed it into the pile that represented the boys and Theresa. They let out a little cheer. "After Theresa finds a landscaper and a pool guy, she can use those same computer skills to plan your vacation!"

"What about the pennies still left?" Tommy asked.

"Those are the second most important ones, Tommy. Those you use for you, your physical health, learning, and your planning sessions for the next level of prosperity. Those will more than pay for the help with the other piles and give you the freedom to achieve more freedom,"

LESSON: If you want more in your life,
you must make room for it.

CHAPTER TWENTY-NINE
The Old Man's Final Lesson

Several months had gone by since the Old Man had passed away and Tommy missed him sorely. He had lived long enough to see Tommy start a family, grow his business, and even make his first few investing mistakes, but Tommy still felt his time with the Old Man had been unfairly cut short.

He used to get upset with the Old Man because he would always laugh when Tommy shared the details of his investing errors with him. The Old Man explained to him that the only way to learn from a mistake and not repeat it was to analyze it clearly.

This was impossible to do when you are deeply upset. Tommy soon noticed that when he learned to laugh at his mistakes, what he had done wrong became obvious, even though he hadn't been able to see that when he was still angry.

The Old Man had taught Tommy that the quickest way to change your state from an unproductive state to a productive and helpful state was to laugh. Laughing was a good way to 'clear the deck' and to think clearly again. He learned that trying to analyze a situation when you are angry only makes the problem worse and the solution more elusive.

Tommy also realized how much the Old Man had taught him outside of his actual lessons, which was also a lesson. The Old Man taught him to always be learning and not to limit his learning opportunities to specific times.

Soon, Tommy's mind returned to the question that had been haunting him (and everyone else) since the Old Man died. Why had the Old Man left Tommy all his money and possessions?

The Old Man had relatives to leave his money to (they would have loved that), why not them?

It would have made more sense if Tommy had been struggling, because of course the two were close, but by then, Tommy was doing quite well, and the Old Man knew it because he had watched closely as his lessons manifested themselves in Tommy's life. Truthfully, as grateful as Tommy was for his unexpected inheritance and the gesture, he was a tiny bit insulted.

Did the Old Man think Tommy wouldn't continue to prosper? Hadn't the Old Man taught him of the dangers of easy and unearned money? Tommy wasn't the only one perplexed by his inheritance. He had listened to more than one of his fellow citizens grumble about how cheap and miserly the Old Man was. "He never gave me a nickel, and I asked nicely!" was a common refrain.

He had witnessed the truth of this many times over himself. The Old Man's reputation as a cheapskate was well-deserved indeed, but it still ran completely contrary to his own experience with the Old Man. The Old Man had never denied him his time, knowledge, or even his patience. The Old Man had been exceedingly generous with Tommy, but it seemed, with no one else. The Old Man even saw fit to give him the money he so often denied everyone else.

Tommy smiled as he realized his old friend was an enigma, he was both an open book and inscrutable at the same time! He had shared everything with Tommy and nothing with anyone else. The question that had been rattling around Tommy's brain so loudly for months now was, why?

"Why me?" Tommy muttered to himself for the millionth time since the Old Man had passed.

He rose out of his chair and crossed the Old Man's living room. He had given most of the Old Man's things to local charities because his family had shown no interest and even scoffed at him when he offered.

The last task left was the one he dreaded the most. The Old Man's desk had been his epicenter. He sat there most of the time when he was teaching Tommy. This was where he filled notebook after notebook with numbers and ideas. Tommy so revered the Old Man that, in Tommy's mind, the chair he had occupied for so long was like a throne.

In all the years he had visited the Old Man, he had never once sat in the chair. The Old Man never forbade it, but he never offered it to him either. Tommy never felt worthy of sitting in the chair, until now.

As he settled into the comfortable chair, he surprised himself with a hearty laugh. He instantly felt his state of mind change from melancholy and grief to one of fond remembrance and nostalgia. He laughed again as he realized that this was another of the Old Man's lessons manifesting itself in Tommy. The Old Man had taught him to use laughter to improve his state to a more productive one conducive to learning something new.

His new mood vanished almost as quickly as it had arrived when Tommy realized that no more of those valuable lessons would be coming. He opened the top drawer of the desk and was surprised to find it nearly empty. It contained only a single envelope with a single word across the front, "Tommy." He was excited about the prospect of one more lesson as he knew the Old Man was not likely to just leave some emotional note for the heck of it. He took a deep breath and removed a single page from the envelope.

Across the top of the page in huge letters, was the word "WHY?!" Tommy smiled as he considered the fact that if he had to describe his old friend using only punctuation marks, it would be a large question mark followed by an exclamation point.

The letter started, "Tommy, by now you have had enough time to figure out why I didn't leave anything to my relatives. I know you remember the lessons about easy money. To them, it would have been very easy money, unearned and undeserved. It would have fled their presence almost immediately and left their lives in worse shape than before. They would have resented me more then, than I am sure they do right now for not giving it to them.

"As you know, many of our neighbors came to me over the years asking for money. I didn't give it to them then, so you can't be too surprised that I didn't give it to them now either.

"You could easily conclude that I left it to you simply because you and I were close, and I ran out of other options, but in your heart, you know that isn't true. You sense that, don't you?"

The Old Man had always possessed an almost uncanny gift for knowing exactly what Tommy was thinking. It was as if the Old Man had a map of Tommy's brain and could see precisely where Tommy's thoughts were headed before Tommy did. Tommy laughed out loud again as he said to himself, "Of course he had a map, he drew it himself!" The Old Man had always emphasized not just the facts, but the process of finding the facts as well.

"You might also have considered that I left you the money because I thought you needed it.

Once again, you sense that is also not true, don't you?

"Why?!" the Old Man asked. "Why did I leave the money to you? The answer is quite simple, and I ask you to consider this to be my final lesson to you, son: I left it to you because you were the only one to ask me for my wisdom instead of my money.

"P.S. "You know exactly what to do with it."

Tommy sat in the Old Man's chair for nearly an hour as he digested the both the lesson and the fact that the Old Man had called him "son," something he had never done while he was alive. The longer he pondered, the more profound he realized this lesson was, and how perfect it was for a final lesson.

He went to his car and retrieved the notebook he always had nearby. He tucked the letter neatly into his inside jacket pocket. It had instantly become his most prized possession. As the Old Man had taught him to do when a lesson was complete, he summarized the lesson into an easy to remember saying:

If you ask a wealthy man for his wisdom instead of his wealth, you will end up both wise and wealthy.

If you ask a wealthy man for his wealth instead of his wisdom, you will end up neither wise nor wealthy.

CHAPTER THIRTY
The First Class

Tommy was quite pleased, but still nervous. Tonight, he was teaching the first 'prosperity' class at the community center. It marked the beginning of the things he wanted to do once he had accumulated enough wealth for himself and his family. The Old Man had emphasized giving back as being the ultimate reason for achieving true prosperity.

Tommy had always agreed in theory, but this would be the first time he would experience the feeling for himself. Of course, he had given people advice over the years and helped many people individually to start businesses or solve financial problems. This class would be the first time he helped a group of people in a more formal setting.

Twenty people had signed up for the class, and by the time Tommy closed the door to start the class, there were fifteen people sitting in the classroom. He had hoped for more, but this would be a good start.

Before they arrived, he had filled the large chalkboard in the front of the room with financial terms. He covered the entire board with random words like debt, interest, assets, liabilities, IRAs, 401ks, stocks, bonds, options, mortgages, rent, etc. In all, he wrote on the board over a hundred terms, some of them common, some more advanced. He was aiming for a specific reaction and he got it.

"For crying out loud!" one man in the front cried out loud. "I don't know what most of those words mean."

As the class settled in and sat down, Tommy addressed them. "Thank you all for coming tonight, I know there are other things you might rather do than go back to school. I know it has been years since graduation for most of you. You may also have unpleasant memories of school, and this board probably isn't helping.

"I apologize for that, but by the time you complete this course, all of these terms will not only make sense to you, they will likely excite you a bit. The main reason that most folks never reach the level of wealth and prosperity they desire is because they never learn the language of money.

"Money concepts are not adequately taught in schools, and most of what is taught is either wrong or incomplete. That is what we are going to correct. Knowing the terms and concepts will set you up to start moving forward towards your goals, even if you have been stalled for a while."

Tommy turned to the board and began to erase all the words written there. He left only two words on the board. He left the words "debt" and "interest." The class seemed visibly relieved to see the rest of the words vanish for now. Two words seemed a lot more manageable than the more than a hundred he'd started with.

He began, "To start our class, we will learn the definition of some basic financial terms, terms that all of us are familiar with already.

"The problem is not that people don't understand what debt means or what interest means. The problem is that most people have the poor person's meaning or perspective on what these words mean, and that makes all the difference in the world."

He continued, "When I say the word debt, is your reaction good or bad?" The class was nearly unanimous. "Bad!" they said in unison.

"How about interest?"

The reaction was the same. "Bad!" they all said, but for one voice in the rear of the room that disagreed. He heard a single "good" even through the chorus of "bad." He knew there was at least one person in the room who was already on the path to prosperity.

"How many people here feel like they are already on a path to prosperity?" Tommy asked.

Only one hand went up, as the students looked around the room to see if anyone raised their hand. Only the man who had answered "good" in the back row raised his hand. They all looked at him. Tommy nodded at the man in acknowledgement and he put his hand back down.

"Why did that man say that debt and interest were good, while the rest of you said they were bad?" Tommy asked.

One man in the front row volunteered, "Because it is impossible to get ahead when you have debt and pay a lot of interest." The group nodded and murmured a few assents.

This was exactly what Tommy suspected. He was going to be able to help these folks, he was sure of it now. Tommy pointed to the gentleman in the back row and asked him, "Please tell the rest of the class in one word why you said debt was good and not bad, sir."

"Leverage" the man replied instantly.

"Excellent," Tommy praised him. "You see, the problem is not that most people don't know what debt is, the problem is that most people misuse debt. Debt is like a firearm. In the right hands, it is a tool for protection and safety. In the wrong hands, it a tool for violence and danger. Most people who struggle financially misuse debt. They use it in a way that damages their financial future, when they could be using it to advance their dreams and goals by using it as leverage, as our friend in the back so rightly told us. The problem is most people use their credit as a tool for accumulating bad debt- debt that you personally must pay off, and generally results from buying things that go down in value after we buy them.

"We end up paying full price, plus interest, for things that become worthless quite quickly. As the gentleman right here said, it is nearly impossible to become wealthy if you have a lot of this type of debt. Who in this room has some of this type of debt?" Tommy asked.

Just as he expected, every hand but one went up. He knew the man in the back wasn't likely carrying this type of debt. He also knew that the man was likely using debt to leverage investments, probably real estate.

Everyone noticed the man was the only one, but Tommy felt the need to clarify. He pointed to the man in the back and said, "Before we go any further, I want to ask my friend in the back a question: "Sir, if you had to guess, besides myself, who in this room has the most total debt?" The man knew why Tommy asked that exact question, and he raised his hand with a smile. The rest of the room was visibly confused, as he hadn't raised his hand when they did.

Tommy explained, "The man in the back there isn't carrying the consumer debt we talked about, but he is likely carrying substantial amounts of another type of debt, debt which he uses as leverage. The difference between his debt and yours is that his debt pays for itself and you pay for yours with your futures."

After giving the class a moment or two to digest that simple but significant point, Tommy continued. "What people like me, and the gentleman in the back, use debt for, is to leverage our own money and to buy bigger investments than we could buy with just our own money. For example, I often buy rental real estate. Typically, I use around 20% of my own money and 80% of the bank's money to buy a property. So, if I buy a $100,000 property, I owe $80,000 on it.

Who pays that debt?"

"You do" answered a few students.

"No, when I rent these properties out, the tenants pay rent, and I use the rent payments to make the mortgage payments and keep the rest after expenses.

"The amount left over isn't usually a large amount, but it is usually a fair percentage of what I personally put into the property myself. The bigger point is that it is not me who pays the debt, the debt pays for itself with the money it earns."

The man in the back row nodded knowingly.

"If you buy $80,000 worth of "stuff," who pays for that? You do. If you buy $80,000 worth of an actual asset, something that earns money, the asset pays for the debt and multiplies the power of your own money. Once you get further along, there will be opportunities to buy assets with none of your own money, isn't that an exciting idea?"

The class was unanimous, "Yes!" they all said.

Tommy had been watching their emotions as he talked. They went from slightly sad and quiet as he was talking about consumer debt to more curious and finally even happy as he talked about buying assets instead. He was making progress towards changing how people saw terms like "debt" and "interest" and he was well pleased. He knew the Old Man would be proud that he was teaching not just one young kid, but over a dozen adults who really needed the help.

He was about to end the class, as he felt this was a good stopping place. He had covered one of the most important points and the class seemed receptive; he was hopeful that most would return the following week and he didn't want to overwhelm them on the first night. His strategy would be to cover one or two concepts each week and then incorporate them into future lessons when he was sure they fully understood them.

The class, however, wasn't quite done yet. One person piped up and asked, "What about interest? Why is that good and not bad?"

Tommy had forgotten about the second term as he was so wrapped up in the first. He didn't want to keep them too late, so for now, he gave a short but truthful answer. "Whether interest is good or bad depends on whether you are paying it or receiving it, but of course there is more to it than that and we will cover that more in our next session together."

LESSON: Bad debt is debt you have to pay yourself.
Good debt pays for itself.

CHAPTER THIRTY-ONE
The Second Class

Tommy was pleased as he counted heads while his new students filed into the classroom. Not only did it appear that all the students from last week had returned, but there were four more students this week. It seemed that several of his students brought friends with them this time.

This development was very encouraging for Tommy, as it made him think that people were receptive to his ideas and that gave him hope.

He had planned to teach about interest this week as a follow-up to the previous lesson on debt, but several of his students asked him to instead discuss another topic. They had read an internet article about how much money a person needed to be able to retire, and they had concerns and questions about what they read.

After making sure the rest of the class was fine with the curriculum change, Tommy decided to address this new topic, since it was one he intended to cover fairly soon anyway. He knew from experience that people tend to pay more attention when they are learning what they want to learn.

"Okay, let's talk about that article. How much did the article suggest a person needed to retire?" Tommy asked, though he had a fairly good idea because he had read many similar articles himself.

"Two million dollars," came the answer. Tommy both heard and felt the collective groan from the class when the number was spoken aloud. He understood the logic of the large number, and the logic was sound in theory, but incomplete in practice. He knew this subject was potentially sensitive.

It was important to make sure his students were hopeful about their futures, and huge numbers like this were not conducive to hope, especially when most of the people reading these articles had but a small percentage of those huge amounts currently available to them. Two million seems impossibly far away to a person who has no money at all or had only recently began to accumulate it and was miles away from having millions of dollars set aside for retirement.

"Who in here feels completely confident that they will have two million dollars in retirement funds accumulated by the time they reach retirement age, let's say at sixty-five?" Tommy asked the class.

As he expected, no hands went up. He could feel the collective mood of the group deteriorate almost immediately. The desire to learn diminishes when folks feel like they are learning for nothing, that what they learn will not help them.

"Good news!" He shouted, startling several of his students. "You do not need two million dollars to retire!"

He paused for a moment, so his students could allow a small sense of relief to come over them and to get their attention so that he could help them realize a more realistic view of retirement planning, a much more hopeful view than most articles of this type engendered among their readers.

"Without getting too deep into anyone's personal finances, let me just ask you, would everyone here be able to survive on an income of around $40,000 a year? I know it is not a huge income, but could you survive on it, if you didn't have any huge debts?"

Most of the classes' hands went up, though a few openly groaned.

"Okay, let's assume that you could survive on that amount, though my goal through this class is to make sure none of you have to live on that little. I intend for all of you to enjoy much more prosperity than that, but we have to start somewhere, so let's start with surviving."

"What I am trying to teach you is that retirement is not necessarily an age or a certain lump sum of money. It is more about having a certain amount of income that comes to you, regardless of whether you go to work or not, at a job or business. That is what retirement really is, it is a level of passive income, income that provides for your basic expenses. Does that make sense?" Tommy addressed the class.

Everyone nodded, and Tommy could sense a slight elevation in their collective mood as he started to erase the huge dollar figure from their worried minds.

"Okay, now let's start to break down that $40,000 income. There is a trailer park a few streets over from the high school. Is everyone familiar with it? In that trailer park, there are multiple trailers that cost $40,000 brand new and much less slightly used. Because our school district is highly rated statewide, the rents of those trailers ranges from $800-1000 per month for a three-bedroom trailer."

Tommy continued. If you could survive on $40,000 per year, that breaks down to a little over
$3300 per month. Does that sound about right?" Tommy paused for a moment to make sure they were following him so far.

Several students nodded in agreement, so he continued, "If you owned five of these trailers outright and averaged $900 per month rental income from them, how much would that be?

Tommy asked the class

"$4,500 per month" several students answered

"How much would it cost you to buy five of these trailers?" Tommy asked. "Around $200,000." Came the answer.

"Not two million dollars?" When several students laughed out loud at the simple logic of Tommy's lesson, he continued, "Of course there are several other factors involved, but the general idea is powerful, isn't it? Two million seems impossible, but how many of you think you could somehow accumulate that much money, given some time, and of course, some excellent lessons about money?"

All his students raised their hands, and Tommy knew for sure that their mood was much better than when they entered the classroom earlier that evening, and that gave him a lot of satisfaction. He knew the facts and concepts were important, but helping people get into a more hopeful state was equally as important to their eventual success and prosperity.

Tommy shared some more ideas with the class. He talked to them about other passive income sources. He talked about things like royalties from intellectual properties like books and songs written.

He talked to them about stocks that pay dividends, bonds that pay interest, and even the idea of working after retirement on projects like owning a small business doing something they enjoyed, but that made money. The general idea he was trying to convey to them was that being able to retire was not a pipe dream, but an increasingly likely event. His message was one of hope, not despair.

Often, folks that write articles like the one they were discussing mean well, but their penchant for throwing around huge dollar figures can backfire. This can discourage instead of inspire their readers, though it is not their intention to do so.

As the class adjourned for the night, several of Tommy's students came to him and thanked him. They told him they were glad they came. They relayed how worried they had been for many years at the prospect of working an entire lifetime to end up on government assistance in their old age. They were looking forward to more lessons and promised to bring more friends next week. Tommy couldn't have been happier, this was what he had always hoped for.

LESSON: Retirement is not an age or a dollar amount, it is a passive income sufficient to pay basic expenses without working.

CHAPTER THIRTY-TWO
The Treasure Map

The first few classes had been going well and Tommy was pleased with the enthusiasm his students displayed. They seemed genuinely engaged and eager to learn more, which is a gratifying thing for any teacher to experience. They had talked about debt and some ideas about retirement. Tommy tried to make a point of giving his students a slightly different perspective on topics they discussed.

The idea was not just to teach concepts and facts, but to encourage them to take another look at virtually every situation they encountered, as that was one of the more powerful 'secrets' of the wealthy and prosperous, looking at the same things everyone else sees, but from a different angle than everyone else. Tonight, he was going to take that concept just a little further than usual.

"Tonight, we are going to talk about everyone's favorite topic, taxes." Several of his students pretended to get up to leave, prompting a stern look and a chuckle from Tommy.

"I know, I know, no one ever wants to talk about the tax system because it is daunting, boring, and most people think of taxes as one of the worst things about living in such a prosperous country.

"Also, and this is not a coincidence, most people in this prosperous country of ours end up broke after working hard for a lifetime." Tommy's students settled down a bit and this statement, though not new to them, had a sobering effect.

"The reason most people hate taxes and even the discussion of the topic is that they have a fundamental misunderstanding of what the tax code represents. We have all seen the politicians using the massive pile of papers that comprise our current tax code as a prop to make some point. We all groan when we think of the complexity of that system.

"The biggest secret of the wealthy that I am going to teach you people is this: To the wealthy and the truly prosperous among us, this tax code does not represent some huge pile of bureaucracy or 'red tape' or even a huge headache on April 15th of each year. To the wealthy, this tax code is actually a treasure map!"

Tommy let those words filter themselves through his students' well-developed nonsense detectors. Predictably, within about thirty seconds, several of his students verbally expressed their doubts about the authenticity of this "secret." One even suggested, with utter sincerity, that Tommy was making a bad joke. He let them express themselves for a few more minutes until he was sure that all of them were of the same mind, that he was nuts. Once they were all on the same page, he could continue with his lesson.

Tommy explained that to the average worker, the system that taxed him more than the investor or business owner was simply unfair and onerous, a conspiracy of the rich who make the rules and laws to hold him and the rest of the working class down. As he was saying this, he saw several of his students nod in agreement.

Just as he suspected, that false and harmful sentiment was just as prevalent among these folks as it was among the general population. Many other well-meaning self-help authors and even leading politicians promoted and supported this faulty perspective, some for their own gain, and some out of ignorance.

"Simply put, highly taxing the working class is a huge flashing sign, a guidepost. It is a warning sign to all who see it. It is telling you that the path you are currently on does not lead to prosperity. It is effective, it shows people that they should be going somewhere else.

"You can stay here if you like, but it is going to become increasingly uncomfortable for you if you do. Like a minimum wage job, the employee tax rates shouldn't be a permanent place for citizens to reside. Just as low wages inspire folks to educate themselves and improve their skills, high taxes inspire people to seek better sources of income. Not coincidentally, these same alternative sources of income happen to be the ones proven to lead to wealth and prosperity anyway.

"Almost no one becomes prosperous through highly taxed earned wages other than athletes and entertainers. The few ordinary citizens who become wealthy while remaining employees do so by gradually transforming those wages into other income sources. The wages themselves never amount to much because of the high tax rates applied to them.

"If you ever aspire to a life beyond struggle and poverty, you must consider a high tax rate as a flame about as tall as your legs. It should be burning your butt every day. Getting out of the high tax burdens imposed on working people should absolutely be your highest priority.

"Why would the government be pushing people out of those high brackets? Wouldn't the greedy government want people paying the higher rates? The simple answer is: No, they do not want that. What the government really needs, and what we should all desire for our country, is for our tax base itself to grow. What that means is that we need more people making more money and paying taxes on those larger amounts, even though the actual rates are lower.

"When a person seeks to remove himself from the burdensome tax brackets of the working class, there are two main ways he can do that: He can start a business directly, or he can invest in the business ventures of someone else. These businesses are the lifeblood of our economy.

"These businesses provide jobs for people. They provide tax revenues for the country, the states, and even the cities they operate in. Many bigger companies are publicly traded and pay dividends to their shareholders. This provides more opportunities for people to make money in ways other than physical work, which is important.

"Investment opportunities are a way for more people to prosper without having to compete with others for physical jobs. Where would the elderly and the retirees in our country be without investment incomes?

"What our tax system really does for the observant and the wise is provide a map towards prosperity. As a bonus, it provides incentives along the way that act as accelerators towards that wealth. If you learn just enough about how different incomes are taxed, you can multiply your wealth in ways that working a regular job simply will never accomplish.

"If we choose to make investments in real estate, for example, we can defer and delay paying taxes on profits indefinitely. There are perfectly legal ways to make a huge profit on the sale of a piece of real estate and not pay any taxes on that sale simply by rolling that money into another piece of real estate, which is likely what you were planning to do anyway.

"Consider the tax burden of a six-figure employee earned income level. The difference between that and the zero-tax liability burden of a real estate exchange is easily between ten thousand and thirty thousand dollars. Think about the difference in effort put forth between an annual salary of six figures and the purchase and sale of a piece of real estate that yields the same amount of money.

"The same incentive system applies to other investments like stocks and bonds. The tax system also looks favorably on profits from these activities as well. Depending on how long the investments are held, they can be taxed as either short-term or long-term capital gains.

Dividends are also usually taxed at lower rates than earned income.

"Anyone determined to ever achieve any measure of prosperity or wealth must quickly and permanently abandon the notion that our tax system is a way for the rich and the powerful to control or oppress the rest of us. It is simply nonsense.

"Nearly every wealthy person in our nation became wealthy through some combination of investing in the stock market, building a business, or investing in real estate.

"The same rich and powerful did not construct the tax system, they simply devised ways to use it become prosperous. The rest of us should learn what they did and aspire to do the same as they did. Think about it, even if the tax rates for the working class of people in this country were zero or nearly zero, would the working class end up wealthy just from their earnings?

"No, they would eventually become too old to work. Eventually everyone ages or becomes too ill to continue the job they have. If they fail to invest or build businesses or acquire real estate, it matters not how little they pay in taxes, they will stop earning and burn any savings they have in a very short time.

"Without the incentive-based tax system we have, the number of Americans ending their lives in poverty would be much higher, as hard as that may be to believe. It is far too high now, and one of the biggest reasons it is still so high, even with the treasure map we have in front of us, is that there are far too many of us who do not see the map on the wall.

"It is right there in plain sight. We look all over for the big 'secrets' to wealth, while we openly complain and bitch about the biggest secret there is right in front of our noses, the U.S. tax system."

---

*LESSON: The tax system is a treasure map,
follow it to prosperity*

CHAPTER THIRTY-THREE
Getting Started

Tommy and his class had spent several weeks talking about some of the terms and ideas that are important for learning to invest and achieving wealth and prosperity. Tommy knew that many folks went as far as reading a few books and learning the language and basic terms of personal finance.

What happens with most people, however, is that they read the books, learn the terms, and then get nervous and do nothing substantial with the information. Soon, the idea of prosperity fades from the forefront of their minds and they return to settling into lives of mediocrity and frustration.

Tommy was determined that his students would not follow that path. He also knew that they were not ready to start making investment decisions yet. If they were to start making moves prematurely, they would likely make mistakes that might discourage them from future ventures.

He decided that he would treat them like any other team, he would teach them to practice the processes and procedures they would need to master to achieve the financial freedom they all desired.

"Okay class, we have a lot to cover tonight so let's get started right away. Get your notebooks out. I am going to give you guys an assignment to complete for next week's meeting. The first thing I want you to do will sound a bit odd but, trust me for a minute. I want every one of you to go home and clean the heck out of one small space.

"You will need room for a desk, a chair, a computer and a printer. You probably already have these things, but I want you to repurpose them for our projects.

"You need a space that is not shared with everything else you are already doing. You need a 'prosperity' desk, a place that you use strictly for purposes of making and executing your plans to become financially free. Until you take steps like this, everything we talk about here is just talk. This is not an academic exercise we are engaging in with these classes. I do not come here just to toss around theories and ideas.

"Once you have this space prepared, you are going to use it right away to make sure it works effectively for you. I want every one of you to look for and find a property for sale within a mile of your homes. I want you to write down the list price. I want you to figure out how much a 20 percent down payment would be and what the mortgage payment would be for the remaining balance.

"Then I want you to find out what the taxes are on that property, which is often in the listing somewhere. I also want you to figure out how much the insurance costs for this property are.

This is also often found in the listing. If not there, you can probably get the information from the real estate agent or estimate it with a little bit of research.

"After you get these basic numbers together, I want each of you to simply make a really basic analysis. I want you to put the list price at the top, then subtract the down payment amount, then write down the estimated mortgage payment for the remaining amount. Add to that monthly payment the monthly amount of the taxes and the insurance. This will give you a pretty good idea of what this property would cost each month to maintain.

"Next, I want you to check out the rental listings in that same area. Look for rental properties that are similar in size and amenities to your property. Figure out what the average rental cost is in that area for a property like yours.

"Once you have this figure, compare it to your monthly cost. If the monthly cost of your property is higher than the rental amount, this property would have a negative cashflow. If the rental amount is higher than the monthly cost, the property has a positive cashflow. I know this sounds like a lot of work. The first time you do it, it will take a while to complete. After you have done it a few hundred times, you will be able to make most of the calculations in your head almost instantly.

"Any questions?" he asked, knowing that many were coming.

"You want us to do all of this by next week?" Amanda asked.

"Yes, and if you really try, you can finish it before Wednesday." He heard an audible groan from the class.

"I know this seems like a lot, but unless we start making this whole process real to you, it will be just an academic exercise in futility. This will all be just like a movie that makes you feel good for a while and then is gone from your consciousness in a few hours. This is too important to your futures and your families for us not to make it real.

"If it makes you feel any better, the Old Man made me do ten of these same types of analysis the first time. I am giving you guys a break!

"Now, let me summarize the assignment: Create a work space. Find and analyze one property. Everyone got it?"

With another collective groan, the class filed out and Tommy gathered his things. His students didn't realize it, but Tommy knew that the outcome of this assignment would largely separate his students into two distinct groups. The ones who completed the assignment and had lots of questions were the ones who would likely go forward and do well. The other group, the ones who failed to complete the assignment and brought back excuses instead of questions would likely fail and continue to lead lives of frustration and mediocrity.

As much faith as Tommy had in his students, his life experience told him that there would indeed be at least several students in the latter group. Mercifully, many of these students would simply not show up for the next class.

Tommy knew this assignment would be a sorting tool of the most efficient kind, but it was necessary to spend his time only with those who were more serious. Spending time with those who were not committed took valuable time away from those who were committed to going forward.

This was just a sad reality in life. Many folks simply refuse to be helped. They have so closely aligned their own identities with their current financial state that it is nearly impossible to separate one from the other. This exercise tends to set off one of two reactions among people.

Some people get excited and rise to the challenge. Others shrink from it and withdraw from the self-improvement process altogether. Tommy was prepared for next week's class to be interesting, and likely a few students smaller.

*LESSON: Book learning is great,
but learning by doing is better.*

CHAPTER THIRTY-FOUR
Assignment Results

As the class filed in, Tommy observed their faces to try to get a feel for how well they had completed the assignment he had given them. Even more importantly, he was doing a silent head count to see how many students he had lost between last week and now. Until now, his class had had nearly perfect attendance, with very few missing any classes without excellent reasons. As far as he could tell, there were now three students missing, which wasn't a huge surprise.

He knew there would be some attrition caused by pushing his students to take concrete steps towards moving their education from the classroom to the real world. The Old Man had warned him many years ago about this happening. What really did surprise him though, was that Amanda was one of the missing. She had been his best and most engaged and enthusiastic student from the beginning.

He waited a few extra minutes before he stood and crossed the room to close the door so that he could start looking over their assignments. As he grasped the door knob and pulled it closed, he felt it pull back. He turned to see why it wouldn't budge. It was Amanda. She hadn't skipped class after all. She was just late.

She seemed to be carrying a library's worth of papers and was clearly struggling with opening the door and keeping her pile of papers from covering the entire floor at the same time. He released the door knob and helped her straighten her pile of papers. He was genuinely relieved that she had made it and had clearly done the assignment. Truthfully, if he had lost her, he would have doubted his own abilities as an instructor. She was an excellent student and quite bright. If he couldn't help her achieve some measure of prosperity, who could he help?

Amanda took her usual seat in the front row, and Tommy noticed that several other students looked as relieved by her presence as he was.

"Did everyone complete their assignment? Did everyone at least complete some or most of it?" Tommy asked.

They all nodded, some with a bit more emphasis than others, but they all appeared to have completed some of what he asked, and that was a good sign. Tommy pointed to the two remaining empty seats. "Look at those empty chairs, for they hold a lesson in them. The sad fact is, not everyone will see this journey through to the end with us.

"Even with all the information, all the encouragement, and all the opportunities available to us all, some folks are simply not ready or willing to leave where they are to go somewhere new, even if that somewhere new looks amazing. The fear of the unknown is a powerful thing.

"OK, now. Who has a question or comment to share with us?"

Several hands went up, including Amanda. He pointed to a student in the back who had rarely spoken during class to this point but was waving his hand wildly to get Tommy's attention. "Go ahead, Glenn." Tommy said.

"First of all, I want to thank you for making me do this. My wife is thrilled with me. My house looks amazing!" The class laughed and nodded.

"Second, I want to share this picture with you. It is my new office space," Glenn said as he approached the front of the class to hand Tommy a large picture of a simple chair and desk with a computer and printer on it. The space was small and simple, but clean and clear, and it looked like it had a purpose to it. Tommy was impressed. He wasn't expecting pictures.

"Third, I did as you asked. I found a property a few blocks from my house that was for sale.

I did the research like you said and I made this analysis here. My wife helped a lot with it. I think cleaning the house really got her attention!" Glenn continued as he handed Tommy a typed paper with the words "Cashflow Analysis" across the top of it. "My wife was so excited, we did three more just like it." He handed Tommy three more reports.

Glenn sat down after delivering his report to the class, and Tommy gave him hearty applause, which the class soon joined. Glenn smiled broadly and was openly emotional. Several of the students sitting near him patted him on the back in support and congratulations.

Several more students shared similar stories, and Tommy was struck by the fact that not one of them complained about the assignment. He had prepared himself to handle a fair amount of griping but was glad that those preparations had been for nothing. He had underestimated his students' determination and dedication. His lessons, or more accurately, the Old Man's lessons, had reached them as deeply as he had hoped they would.

Amanda spoke last. She showed Tommy a picture of a pile of trash at the curb in front of her house. "My husband says he wants to buy you a drink, by the way." The class laughed.

Next, she showed him a picture like the one Glenn had shown him, of her new office space. She had converted an extra bedroom into a home office. She had a whiteboard mounted on one wall and a large desk with computer, and several filing cabinets. Like she always did, she had taken this lesson to heart and exceeded what was asked of her.

Tommy was very proud. Then she handed him a stack of papers. She explained that there were seventeen properties for sale near her house. She had done the cashflow analysis on each one of them. She had sorted them in order of cashflow potential. On top of the pile was the one with the biggest positive cashflow and the one on the bottom was the one with the biggest negative cashflow.

After a well-deserved round of applause from Tommy and the rest of the class, Amanda sat down, and several students raised their hands with questions.

One of his students told him that he had done an analysis on a condominium unit. The positive cashflow seemed pretty good and the student was rightly wary. Tommy said,"Go back to the listing and look for something called an HOA fee. HOA stands for Home Owner's Association. An HOA fee is something the condominium management collects from the owners to use for the maintenance of the grounds of the property. It pays for things like landscaping, swimming pool maintenance, and maintenance of the building's exterior. It is collected on either a monthly, quarterly, or annual basis.

"This fee is usually disclosed in the listing. Once you find the number, you simply calculate the monthly cost and add it to your monthly cost calculations. Before buying a condo unit as an investment, it is also important to check the HOA rules concerning investment rentals.

"Some do not allow them at all and others limit the number of units that can be rented. If you intend to rent out a condo unit, make sure you will be allowed to do so before buying.

"Tommy spent another hour answering questions about different types of mortgages, owner financing, and all manner of questions regarding taxes, property managers, etc. He was pleased and even a bit surprised by the level of engagement.

"His class had been interested before, but now he sensed that they were really intrigued and encouraged. They were making the transition from book learning to real life experience-based learning and that was exciting. He was almost disappointed that he would now be sending them back to book learning, but he knew he had no choice.

"I am very proud of all of you for how well you carried out these assignments. Truthfully, I was a little worried, but you guys really came through and I am thrilled to see you start to apply what we have learned here to real life. It is truly exciting to watch.

"Now, I have another assignment for you. This one is easy compared to last week's assignment. I want every one of you to go to the bookstore and buy a book from the personal finance section. Buy one book on either beginning real estate or beginning stock trading. If you would like me to recommend a book, I can do that, but I prefer that you go and choose a book that appeals to you. Buy one book, read it, and be ready to discuss it next week."

Amanda spoke up, "Wait. If we all buy different books, how will you know which ones we buy and need to discuss? What if we all buy totally different books?" The rest of the class seemed to share her concern.

"I have been to that bookstore many times, Amanda. There isn't a book there I haven't read at least once. Some of them I have read several times. Don't worry about me, worry about finding a book that interests you."

LESSON: There is no substitute for hands on learning. Books and classes will only get you so far. At some point, you must apply what you learn.

Chapter Thirty-Five
The Importance of Giving

Tommy and his class had spent a few classes reviewing some of the books they had been reading and going into more detail on the cashflow analysis reports they had been doing.

Tommy was pleased that many of them would indeed use his lessons to achieve a good measure of prosperity with what he had taught them. He had started discussing with them what types of things they would do once that prosperity became a reality for them.

At the end of the last class, Tommy had asked his students to spend some time thinking about and planning what kinds of things they would do once they achieved some wealth and prosperity. He knew that most of them had heard other teachers and authors ask them to do this same exercise as a sort of positive affirmation activity.

Many self-help authors encourage their readers to visualize all the good things they could do with more money, because it is a way to help those readers create for themselves a strong "why," a reason that motivates them when times get tough. Thinking about the good things one can do with wealth is an excellent exercise, without doubt.

Having a strong "why" is essential when creating a plan for one's future. Nothing is a better incentive for good people than the prospect of being able to help others. Tommy asked the class to share with him some of the goals they had come up with, so they could vocalize them, which also helped make those ideas more real.

Most of his students offered similar goals. Many wanted to help family members who were struggling. Many wanted to help feed the hungry folks in their community. Some wanted to spend time doing volunteer work. A few wanted to help find solutions to the homeless crisis.

Tommy acknowledged that these were all noble and worthy goals and he praised his students for their good intentions. Then he decided to push this idea just a little farther to help his students really grasp the importance of giving, not just as the academic lesson they just had.

"How many of you, with a show of hands, are already doing these things right now?" Tommy asked, as he raised his own hand.

As he had feared, only two hands went up. The discomfort among the class was palpable.

Tommy could feel the collective mood in the classroom deteriorate quickly. He expected that to happen, and it was an important step in this process. He wanted to make them feel a little discomfort.

He never intended for his classes to be feel-good sessions. He intended for them to lead his students towards a more prosperous existence, which they could feel good about once they were on their way, but he knew that sometimes a little tough love was necessary.

"OK, put your hands down. Listen, I wasn't trying to hurt anyone's feelings or single anyone out, but this is a very important concept for you guys to grasp, so bear with me for just a minute.

"Has anyone in here ever been on any sort of fitness routine or diet?" Tommy asked as he raised his own hand. This time, nearly every hand went up, and the mood lightened a bit.

"OK, has anyone ever heard of 'starvation mode'?" Amanda, one of his best students raised her hand and he pointed at her to answer.

"Starvation mode is when someone actually eats too little trying to lose weight, and their body goes into a panic and starts storing everything they eat to store energy, so it doesn't starve. It is like an emergency mode. It makes losing any further weight nearly impossible to accomplish." she answered.

"What is the solution?" Tommy asked.

"Stop dieting so hard and eat a little more, so your body can stop panicking." she replied. "Excellent, that is exactly the point I am trying to teach you about money. When you decide to wait until you have enough to share before you start doing things for other people, you are telling yourself that you do not have enough, and your mind and your bank accounts go into 'starvation mode,' you fall back into a scarcity mindset instead of an abundance mindset.

"When starving yourself of food, your body fears that no more food is coming, so it clings to what it gets. When you hold on to every dollar you have, your subconscious believes that no more money is coming, and it shuts down the resources it had been devoting to finding more abundance for you.

"You give up without knowing you gave up. At whatever point you stop giving, you become stuck at that point forever. If you are real lucky, you get to stay there and not fall back. But you will not go forward."

He continued, "If you want more in your life, you have to truly believe there is more for you to get, if you believe there is more for you to get, you must make some room for it. You must let go of some of what you already have. If you cannot let go and make room, you will receive no more. It really is that simple. Think of it like this: Think like a fisherman for a minute. Think of your income as a bunch of fish you just caught.

"Your chunk of money that is for your essential bills is one big fish. You keep that one.

Think of your investment money as another big fish that you keep for yourself. But, the rest of it, the money that is not committed to essential bills or investing is a bunch of little fish. These fish you throw back. Catch and release. You return them to the big pond, the economy. You send them back into the world, so they can grow larger. Later, you can catch them again if you like.

"These little fish, these small amounts of money may be the meal that helps someone through a hungry day. They might be the used lawnmower the neighbor kid needs to cut a few lawns and make his first money. They might be the gas a single mom needs to get to work to feed her kids.

"Release these small fish, no matter how small they are, and they will grow somewhere. The more money that is circulating and growing, the more that is available to us later when we need it. Don't think of it as losing money. It is not lost. It is just spending some time helping someone else for a while.

"Because of what you are learning, you will soon have the skills and the confidence to go into the world and get from it as much as you need to do the things you want to do, for yourselves and for others. But first, you must demonstrate to yourself and the world that you can be trusted not to hang onto money you don't really need at that moment in time and are willing to share with those around you.

"Once you and the world are convinced that you can be trusted, money will come more easily to you. People will feel comfortable investing in your ideas, buying your products and your services. Be the fisherman who knows he can go to the pond anytime he likes and pull out all the big fish he needs and will gladly return the smaller ones for others to use or for others to grow themselves. There is plenty to go around, as long as no one tries to hoard and hide away more than they really need."

Tommy finished by asking his class to indulge him in another exercise. He asked every one of them to go home and give away some money. It might only be a few dollars. Maybe buy a few cans of soup and bring them to the local foodbank. Maybe hand some change to a homeless person on the side of the road. Maybe take out a struggling friend to a nice dinner and supportive conversation.

The amount wasn't important. What was important would be the ability to release money, knowing that it could be easily replaced, knowing that we live in a world of abundance if we choose to live there. It is created for each of us by our own actions and thoughts. Doing things like this also helps us to learn what the true purpose of achieving wealth is, which is to acquire the ability to help others. Giving away small amounts of money when we do not have much is simply practice for giving away larger amounts later.

*LESSON: If we do not learn to give,
our ability to receive is compromised greatly.*

CHAPTER THIRTY-SIX
Why Not You? The Hendersons

This was the last meeting with the class. They had decided to break for the summer and resume in the fall. Tommy had considered the class a success. His students had missed very few classes, they had done all the assignments he had given them, and they seemed genuinely engaged in the learning process.

He was hopeful that most of his students would take his lessons to heart and go on to live quite prosperous lives, which for him, was the greatest reward a teacher could receive. The Old Man had given him the knowledge and the tools he needed to do well for himself and his family. There was always the unspoken assumption that Tommy would use what he learned for his own purposes, but also would also do everything he could to teach what he knew to others as well.

Tommy was confident that he was fulfilling his unspoken promise and was a little sad that this class was adjourning, even if just for a few months. Yes, Tommy was feeling good, right up until the moment Amanda came in a few minutes early and took her seat in the front row as she always did. Her head was hanging low, and she was clearly not feeling the same hopefulness for the future that Tommy was feeling.

Tommy immediately sat at the desk next to her to determine the cause of her distress. After a few minutes of gentle prodding she finally blurted out, "I just don't think I can do this!".

Tommy asked gently, "You can't do what?"

"All of this!" she said as she gestured to the chalkboard and her notebook. "It all sounds great in theory, but it is just too much for me."

By that time, the rest of the class had filtered in and taken their seats. They had observed the intense level of the discussion going on, and they were understandably concerned.

Tommy decided that if his best student was having doubts, it was a virtual certainty that the rest of his class had them also. This would be his last chance to send them out into the world with the right attitude. All the knowledge and wisdom in the world are useless without the right attitude implementing them. He decided to tell them a story he hadn't shared with them before.

"By now, all of you are quite familiar with the Old Man, my time with him, and the lessons he taught me. They were obviously the basis for all we learned here. He might have known more about money than anyone I ever met. The things he taught me were essential to where I am today. But, honestly, by the time I had learned everything he taught me, I was doing well, but not breaking any records.

"I was still not totally convinced that I could achieve what I had set out to achieve. Like many of you, I had trouble seeing myself being in a place where money wasn't a real concern anymore. I knew the Old Man had done well, but I also knew he'd had a great mentor himself.

"Shortly after I married Theresa, I met her grandparents. Their names were Fred and Nazil Henderson. When I met them, they had just retired at age 55 and were finishing up the work on their dream home. It was fabulous. It had 5 bedrooms, as many bathrooms, two living rooms, a large shop and a large yard. It was everything they had ever wanted in a home. But the house isn't what was impressive to me. What was impressive was how they got to building that house.

"I was lucky enough to spend a lot of time with them because they lived near us and Theresa was close with her grandparents. I learned that they had married later in life, in their forties.

Both had been married before and had children from previous marriages.

"They had grown up in Mississippi in an area that was fairly poor. They grew up in a time when college educations were rare and even graduating high school wasn't very common. They got married and moved away from their families to start a new life for themselves. They started with nothing but a desire to work hard and provide for their family as best as they could.

"Fred had never gone to college, but he was a brilliant man who could take apart any mechanical device and put it back together without the first manual or blueprint. He could tell what was wrong with most machines by listening to them. He worked for a company that drilled holes for water wells and for testing ground conditions.

"Nazil got a job with the U.S. Post Office and was a mail carrier in her neighborhood for decades. She is the toughest woman I ever met, and never missed work. If she was sick, she went to work. If she was sad, she went to work. Whatever was going on in her life, she went to work and then dealt with whatever needed dealing with afterwards.

"Fred and Nazil made good salaries and were valued employees. A lot of people could make that claim. What made them so special and amazing to mé, was how they handled their money. They didn't have the Old Man helping them. They didn't read money books all day long. They didn't have wealthy relatives giving them advice. They just had good old-fashioned common sense. They used one paycheck to pay their bills. They took the other paycheck and they saved it, just put it away and didn't think twice about buying stuff they didn't need. Their kids had everything they needed, and they never went without. They took nice vacations, and they lived quite well by any standard.

"They always helped others, were generous with their church, and active in their community.

I am telling you all this because I want you to know they didn't have to live like hermits to do well. They simply saved first and then enjoyed the rest.

"Every so often, they would take their savings and buy a piece of land at an auction. They waited until they found a property in an area they knew and bought them when the price seemed right. Sometimes, they bought a chunk of stock in a company they liked and just let it sit and grow in an account somewhere.

"After a few years, when the pieces of land had risen in value, they sold them and bought others that were well located and priced well. Their stocks paid dividends, and they saved those payments as well.

"Eventually, a plot of land came up for sale only a few hundred yards down the road from their house. They had saved enough money to buy the land and build their dream house. Fred and Nazil were hard working people and handy with tools, so they built a lot of the house themselves. Fred rented some machinery and did the sitework himself to save money. By the time the house was completed, it was worth much more than it cost them to build.

"They filled the house with beautiful furniture and it was always filled with friends and family. Every holiday and many weekends were spent there, eating and just talking with family and friends that came from all over to visit.

"After a lifetime of working and saving, the Hendersons not only had their dream home, they retired at 55 and they had a net worth north of seven figures. They never caught any huge breaks, they suffered the same tragedies and hardships that all families do. They had no college degrees, just a boatload of intelligence and common sense.

"They started with nothing and ended up with everything. They didn't start a huge computer company, they didn't invent some new gadget, they didn't really get lucky in any significant way other than meeting each other. They simply made a plan and stuck to it.

"What they did is exactly as we have learned right here in this class. They saved their money by not buying junk they didn't need. They invested in things they understood well, local real estate and companies they were familiar with. When they made a profit, they bought something else. They just kept doing that until they had enough to retire. Then they built their dream house and kept doing the same thing.

"The Hendersons weren't lucky. They had no advantages. They just worked hard, and they just never quit. They were simply unstoppable. They reached financial freedom starting from scratch in around 15 years with no formal education, and without these classes for a head start.

"My question to all of you is this: Why not you? If the Hendersons can achieve all they did with no complicated plan, why can't you do the same?

"Are all of you able to work and make money? Are you able to set aside a few bucks from your paycheck for yourself? Can you read some books to learn about a specific topic? Can you do some basic math to see if something adds up or not? Can you sign your name to a piece of paper? Is there any individual part of this that you cannot physically do?

"Of course not. You say you can't do all of this, and you are right. You can't, at least not all at once. You can put aside a few bucks today. Next week, you can look at the local real estate listings to see if anything looks interesting. Tomorrow, you can watch the business channel to see what the stock market is up to. You can buy a new book. You can talk to a banker about what it would take to get funding for an investment property. You can have coffee with someone who is already doing what you want to do. You can start a small business on weekends to raise money for investing. You can open an online stock account and buy a few shares of something.

"If the Hendersons can be financially free starting from scratch, why not you?"

LESSON: None of what it takes to be financially free is hard if you do one step at a time. You simply must be unstoppable!

CHAPTER THIRTY-SEVEN
Tommy's Dream Spreads

Tommy's class resumed in the fall. He was pleasantly surprised when he had to move his class to a larger room. His class had nearly doubled since the last class in the spring. Some of his students had spent their summer looking for and even acquiring a few rental properties. He had spent a fair amount of his own summer answering questions and meeting with them as they worked on their first few investments.

All their activity and their interest confirmed for him how much this type of education was needed. Given enough information and encouragement, nearly anyone could achieve a fair measure of financial freedom and prosperity. Some could even go on to become super wealthy if they chose to work hard enough.

Tommy spent the first few classes reviewing material from the previous classes to help the new students catch up. Once he felt they were sufficiently up to date, he started teaching more advanced concepts. He taught them about using options to leverage their money in the stock market. He taught them ways to make money from the stocks they already held using options. He taught them to consider alternative forms of passive income like royalties from writing.

He talked to them about building businesses and about eventually getting away from being an employee and instead being an owner and controlling their own income. He taught them about different ways to finance real estate deals. He taught them many things, but the main idea he wanted them to understand was that the big secret to wealth and prosperity is that there is no secret at all.

Everything they needed to learn was readily available. People who had already achieved success using a certain investment vehicle are quite willing to share what they learned along the way. Many write books, teach seminars, teach classes, etc. Any bookstore or library is full of collected knowledge. The internet provides access to nearly every bit of collective knowledge that exists today.

Tommy's classes had become so popular, that he found it necessary to have some of his former students teach other groups of new students. The neighboring town started a class based on his teaching in their own civic center.

Tommy eventually wrote a book that summarized and encapsulated the lessons he'd learned from the Old Man and had been teaching his students. He realized the appetite for helpful knowledge was great, and it was something that our education system routinely overlooked.

Tommy's book became quite popular and was even used in some high school classrooms to teach young people some of the basics of investing and wealth. Tommy and Theresa turned over the control of most of their businesses and real estate to others and focused full-time on delivering their message of financial education and prosperity to as many people as would listen.

Not surprisingly, sharing their knowledge and experience helped them become even more prosperous themselves, which helped them be more able to share with more people. The Old Man had always taught him to look for ways to help people, and not so much for ways to make money. If you help enough people, the money will be there.

LESSON: When we share what we know, we all grow.